CHINA

By Diana Granat and Stanlee Brimberg

SCHOLASTIC
PROFESSIONAL BOOKS

New York • Toronto • London • Auckland • Sydney
Mexico City • New Delhi • Hong Kong

Dedication

To our dear family members, Stan and Robert, and Ellen, Molly and Mae.

Acknowledgments

With thanks to Pearl Zeitz, Edith Gwathmey, Michael Cook, Peni Golden, Sandra Pezzella, and the other teachers at the School for Children who left us their materials and their wisdom; to Ellen Schecter and Jeff McCartney who encouraged us; and to Bank Street's students, whose creativity and hard work are a constant inspiration to us.

Cover design by Pamela Simmons
Interior design by Drew Hires
Maps by GEOSYSTEMS, Columbia, MD
Photo research by Sarah Longacre
Cover Photograph: The Great Wall © Keren Su 1995/FPG International
Interior Photos
Chinese New Year (page 5), Yangtze River (page 12) and Chinese Drum Dancers (page 72): AP Photo/Greg Baker
Taoist Priests/Chinese New Year (page 26): AP Photo/Lee Chuan-hsien
Confucius (page 27): Courtesy, Museum of Fine Arts, Boston
Landscape Painting "He Treasured Ink Like Gold" (page 66): Collection of National Palace Museum, Taipei, Taiwain, Republic of China
Shanghai (page 81): AP Photo/Joe McDonald

ISBN 0-590-76987-1

CONTENTS

INTRODUCTION

How to Use this Book

How you approach this book depends a great deal on your own learning style. Some people open the box, plug in the toaster oven, and make toast. They only refer to the manual when their English muffin is on fire. If that's you, you are probably ready to go right to the first chapter, Geography. You can always check back later on, after you get your feet wet, or when your muffin catches fire. Other learners like to know what their new appliance can do and how it works. If that's you, read on. Then, as you gather steam, study, browse, or skip, as you wish.

There are seven chapters, presented in what we feel is a natural order. An understanding of China's *geography* leads to a sense of why Chinese feel the way they do about life (*philosophy and religion*). These belief systems have been powerful forces in China's *history.* Other chapters include *Language and Writing*, *Painting and Other Art*, *Family and Culture*, and *Modern China*. We suggest you begin with the first two. After that, decide on whatever order best suits your students.

Each chapter has four parts:

1. Goals for the Unit

Previews of relevant concepts and skills you might present to students.

2. Background Information

You can reproduce these sections for students to read or read them aloud to the class. This information will help you to provide the essential connective tissue so that students participating in the activities suggested in the rest of the unit can develop a context for the information they learn, i.e., Big Picture.

For example, making fried rice is a good school activity, but unless it is linked to an understanding of why the Chinese eat so much rice, and how the food preparation techniques are related to issues of scarcity of meat and fuel, it floats free. It's enjoyable, but it may not add to students' knowledge of China and its people.

3. Activities

- Lesson Plans: These are complete or nearly complete.
- Follow-up Activities: To extend the lesson.
- Teaching Strategies: Comments about the benefits and shortcomings of various methods of presentation.

4. Reproducibles

- Pages to accompany the activities.

Planning Your Unit

The experts who designed the curriculum you teach and the editors who put together the books you use have a lot to offer you. But they're trying to anticipate the needs of a wide audience they don't know. *You* are the one who actually brings learning opportunities to your students. Most of us can look at a resource and think, This won't work for Sammy and Catherine, or This is great; I wish I had time for it. The questions and the short discussions that follow here are intended to help you to articulate the considerations that lead all of us to make our teaching choices regardless of the level of planning you're doing.

Who Are We Teaching?

It's common sense that the more you know about your students, the better able you will be to serve their needs and be able to make observations and decisions like these:

- This reading is too difficult for Jesse. How can I support him with it? Maybe he could read it with Frank and they could discuss it as they go along.
- Six of my students are pretty good at decoding, but they think about things very concretely. How can I help them see the moral of this fable? Maybe we could have a short meeting and discuss a few of Aesop's fables together.

Some teachers object to this kind of thinking. They feel that their is job to set the bar height and every student's job is to clear it. But if you know something about what your students know, how they learn, what their temperaments are, their life experience, and how they socialize with each other, you'll be able to decide what is a reasonable height for each child. Children won't give up if the challenges you present can be attained. Then you can raise the bar again. If your sixth-period class reads on average more slowly than your second-period class, don't assign them fifty pages a night. If your seventh-grade class will be insulted by reading a Chinese fable in a picture book, take the time to explain that now they are not merely readers, they are anthropologists. Match the style of presentation to the children.

How Long Should It Last?

Planning our time is among the most difficult tasks teachers face. There's always a tension between the great job we want to do and the calendar, which seems to race by more quickly each year. Sometimes there's little choice: we have to be at Modern China by December. But being realistic about the amount of time we *can* give to each part of that journey determines *how* we're going to present it. Hands-on activities eat up time; reading is much faster. However, if the whole study is done out of a textbook, few students will remember much of it. If children have only hands-on activities, we run the risk of producing learners who know *something* about the topic, but who don't have the bigger picture. Our plans include both reading and hands-on activities.

What Resources Do We Have?

Time is one of our most important resources. Here are some others:

- **Materials:** What's already in the building? What's in the classroom? Books? Pictures? Magazines? What's in the library? What can I beg, borrow, or steal from others?
- **Location:** Am I in a place that lends itself to this study? For example, in New York City, there is a Chinatown, a large Chinese population, hundreds of Chinese restaurants and Asian groceries, plus several museums and cultural organizations dealing with Asia.
- **Money:** What is my budget?
- **People:** Are there people in the community with expertise about some aspect of my curriculum? For example, the librarian is a first-generation Chinese immigrant. Would she like to talk to the class about China? Could she help us with our calligraphy? Could the owner of the local Chinese restaurant arrange for us to see a dish prepared?

How Should We Present the Material?

Our choice of teaching strategies follows from a few essential questions: What's the content? How can I present it in a way that will be interesting and accessible to my students? So here are some further considerations to help answer these questions:

- **Teacher style:** Some teachers are very charismatic, and students love to listen to them talk. Lecture and discussion classes work for them. Others are better as facilitators of small group or individual activities. There are many variations. What works for you?
- **The nature of the experience:** Speaking and listening are the fastest way to communicate information. It's quicker to read about making soup than to make it, more economical to hear about the Great Wall than to visit it. But firsthand experience is clearly different. The closer we are to real experience, the more likely any learning is to stick. So you should try to present material in a variety of ways, including real and contrived experiences, secondary experiences like films and videos, as well as reading, lectures, and discussions.

How Will We Assess What Students Have Learned?

There are a number of assessment instruments, and we use a variety of them to give us a broad picture of what students have learned.

- **Everyday observations:** While this is the most casual, it's still one of the most powerful ways to find out what students know. We see how and how much children talk about curriculum. We look at how—and with what depth and accuracy—they deal with assignments.

- **Short-answer quizzes and tests:** Their benefits are that they are relatively fast to produce, administer, and review. If previewed properly, they help students organize massive amounts of information into chunks, to abbreviate it, sort it, and encode it into memory. In a world of gray areas, our students are at an age at which they're desperate to know what's right and what's wrong; here is one way they are able to do that.

  However, there are otherwise intelligent children who can't find discrete pieces of information on demand. Others panic on tests no matter what. These tests are negative experiences for them. No matter how impressive a student's test average is, it only indicates that that student has the kind of mind to do well on tests.

- **Writing projects:** Essays provide opportunities for children to demonstrate their understanding of concepts. We often assign compositions in which the writer takes the part of a person in the culture being studied and either reports on some aspect of life in that culture, tries to solve some problem using the tools available in that place at that time, or explains his or her response to a historical event.

- **Other kinds of projects:** Students make figures, maps, drawings, and murals; have debates; dress up, write and perform scenes. These require larger chunks of class time, but they are enjoyable and demonstrate mastery of particular aspects of the curriculum.

- **Portfolios:** Many students save their work. But unless that folder of work is revisited often, and unless students use what's in there to make something or to solve something new, it serves only as a record of what the student has done, not what he or she knows. Students should use the material in their folders to present a talk, a play, or in some way chew on what's in there with the benefit of the perspective of time.

What to Teach

For most of us, choices about what we teach are made by our states or localities. Often, these curricula are intelligent, well-conceived, and constructed—but much too long. For example, the sixth-grade social studies curriculum for New York City is Asia. With so much geography, so much history, and such a diversity of cultures, many teachers feel they have no choice but to gallop through the subject. These surveys are the educational equivalents of visiting eight countries in 14 days. For real learning to occur, there must be repetition and redundancy. Ideas need time to sink in, to reinforce themselves as they are encountered over and over again. Therefore, we should all learn how to address what we need for our students, and to learn to take control of what we teach.

We've already thought about time, resources, fit, methodology, and assessment, but how do we deal with the actual content, the what? The following chart, "The Curriculum Planning Sequence," outlines how we plan our curriculum.

The Curriculum Planning Sequence

Definitions	Example	Significance
Concepts: Abstractions that provide ways of sorting information into ideas that are bigger than the specific information.	**1.** Economic system: a set of relationships and procedures which enables goods and services to be distributed.	**1.** Concepts take up less memory than specific information, so an understanding of them enables a person to manipulate ideas without being distracted by details. **2.** They are transferable; for instance, a geography concept, learned in a study about the Civil War, will be useful in other studies and in life outside of school.
Information: The specifics of learning; what we call facts and figures, names and dates, events, accounts, data.	**1.** The Communist Revolution brought a new political and economic order to China under Mao Zedong.	**1.** Provides the specifics that make events different and distinct. **2.** Roots concepts, making them concrete. **3.** It is the stuff of memory, essential for communication of ideas.
Activities: Purposeful endeavors designed to accomplish a goal. Activities require skills.	**1.** Reading and discussing *Animal Farm.* **2.** Making a scrapbook.	**1.** In school, activities are the way students gather and consider, practice using, and demonstrate their mastery of information and concepts.
Skills: Sets of behaviors that enable us to make use of concepts and information.	**1.** Reading a novel (decoding; literal and inferential comprehension) **2.** Participating in a class discussion.	**1.** Skills empower people to make things and to do things. **2.** Skills have personal and economic value.

Concepts

Concepts, also called understandings, are mental constructs. Children usually arrive at school with many of these, especially ones referring to *things*. Other concepts are more abstract; they are ideas for organizing other ideas: an economic system refers to abstractions such as needs, resources, power, and distribution. The younger a child is, the more he or she will need to understand things in a concrete way. Although by the middle school years, most children are ready to encounter abstractions, many still benefit greatly from concrete experiences.

Information

Is there some specific body of information that all children should know today? The notion of a canon is hotly debated. Some educators feel that an emphasis should be put on concepts and thinking skills, rather than on informational content. This important issue should always be discussed and argued. Meanwhile, we have to decide. One answer is that if we can demonstrate the relevance and importance of the information to our students, we're comfortable teaching it.

Other things to think about are: Should you teach all the information in this book? What information should you choose to present? To decide, begin with your state guide and then analyze the considerations in the previous section.

Skills

Let's put aside for a moment the idea that all children should be able to do thus-and-such by a particular age. In order to *get* the concepts and the information, we plan *activities.* Some may be relatively simple, like reading a chapter and answering review questions, and some will be more elaborate, like making a three-dimensional relief map. All of these require some skills. Think about what Maggie has to be able to do just to answer those review questions. She has to read the chapter in a reasonable amount of time; she has to have a strategy; she needs to summarize chunks as she reads, keeping key points in mind; she may need to take notes. The list goes on.

Any way we choose to present content implies acquiring a set of skills. So there are two ways of approaching this task: 1) do a project and directly teach some of the skills students will need to accomplish its goals; 2) design an activity which through content requires students to practice a particular skill, and teach the skill before the students have to do the activity.

The second option raises the question: what skills should children know at what age? Sometimes a group gets to our classes with such serious skills deficits that we can't present certain projects we love. In such a case, we do the professional thing: teach the skills, figure out a suitable modification, or choose another activity. It's up to us to know what's a reasonable stretch and what will end in frustration and failure.

Why Know this Stuff?

Understanding the roles of concepts, information, and skills in activities enables us to make suitable and important decisions for individual students. For example, once we finish reading the Analects of Confucius, students are supposed to paraphrase them, then choose one and illustrate it. If Laura can't paraphrase the sentences, we can simply have other students help her with the paraphrasing part and then, later, give her simpler material to paraphrase. If Ben has difficulty drawing and he hates it, we might encourage him to make a poster with the words of wisdom, but without the picture.

What About Fun?

Many people feel activities that are fun do not provide "serious learning" for middle school students. As we stated above, activities augment and solidify learning. Students who read about Chinese painting may remember little of what they learned. But those who have painted a Chinese-style landscape will always remember the experience.

On the other hand, a good activity should not just be "fun." The activities you choose and the way you modify them for your group should be decided upon only after a consideration of *what you want your students to learn.* A well-designed activity appropriate to the needs of your students will usually feel pretty good to them, even if it doesn't have bells and whistles.

A Note About Written Chinese

Chinese is written using *characters*, a term referring to ideographic units, rather than alphabet-based words. The pronunciation of characters has been transcribed into Western languages using the sound-reproduction systems of Western linguistics.

For many years, one transcription system (or "romanization") was used. It was called Wade-Giles romanization, after its creators. After 1949, linguists in the People's Republic of China developed their own romanization system. In recent years, this newer system, known as *pinyin*, has become standard. However, older books will all use the older Wade-Giles system. In this curriculum guide, the current pinyin system will be used, but the older Wade-Giles form will be given in parentheses the first time the word is used. The only exceptions will be when the older name is so widespread that using the new one will cause undue confusion.

Chinese names and words can seem very intimidating to students. Practice saying them yourself so you can help your students to feel more comfortable. In Mandarin, syllables always end in vowels, *n*, or *ng*. Here is a guide to the approximate pronunciation of Chinese using pinyin.

Sounds	Pronunciation	Examples
Vowels	a=ah e=uh i=ee o=oo (as in look) u=oo (as in food)	Han (Hahn), Tang (Tahng), Shang (Shahng) Deng (Duhng) Jin (Jeen) Song (Soong) Ju (Joo), Chu (Choo)
A single *I*	Following c, s, or z-uh Following ch, sh, or z=	Cixi (Tsuh-syi), Sichuan (Suh-chwan), Yangzi (Yahng-dzuh) chifan (chur-fahn) Shikai (Shur-kai) Zhimin (Jur-meen)
Compound vowels	ao=ow/au yi=ee iu=yo ou=oh	Mao (Mau) Yibin (Ee-been) Liu (Lyo) Ouyang (Oh-yahng)
Consonants	the same as English EXCEPT: c=ts q=ch x=sh z=dz zh=j	 Cixi (Tsuh-syi) Qin (Cheen) Xiaoping (Shyau-peeng) Zedong (Dzuh-doong) Zhou (Joe)

U.S. Department of Interior: Board on Geographic Names. Gazetteer of the People's Republic of China: Pinyin to Wade-Giles, Wade-Giles to Pinyin. Washington: Defense Mapping Agency, July 1979.

Chapter 1

Geography

Goals for the Unit

Concepts

1. Where people live influences the way they live: people both modify their physical environment and are affected by it.
2. In areas of dense population, there is a need for cooperation and for means to resolve conflicts.
3. Natural occurrences can drastically affect life and property.
4. People use the natural resources and the land itself to live.
5. Regions have distinct physical and cultural characteristics.
6. The location of important cities is often based on geographical features that enhance transportation and communication (like rivers, ports, rich farmland).
7. Maps enable us to learn graphically about geography, history, political science, economics, and culture.

Skills

1. Getting information from text; taking notes; answering written questions.
2. Getting information from a speaker; taking notes; rewriting notes.
3. Using maps: political, relief, special purpose, scales of distance, latitude and longitude, direction.
4. Using charts and graphs: reading and interpreting data; using data to answer questions.

Background Information

China's Geography

China's Isolation

China, the fourth largest country in the world, is the largest country in East Asia. Historically cut off from most of its neighbors by natural barriers of ocean, mountains, rain forest and desert, China developed its civilization distinct from other great ancient civilizations in Africa, the Middle East, and Asia. Lands more accessible to China, such as Japan, Korea, and Vietnam, were strongly influenced by its culture. To the north, where no natural barriers existed, China built an artificial barrier: the Great Wall. The Wall was never completely effective, and through the centuries, China had a volatile relationship with the people who inhabited the steppes of north and central Asia. These nomads raised herds of animals for a living, whereas Chinese civilization was based on a settled, agricultural lifestyle. Conflict over land in the border areas was common. When China was strong, it took over land from the nomads. When China was weak, the nomads invaded and conquered parts or all of China.

The Scarcity of Farming Land

China has very little arable (farming) land, but an enormous population. Although China is roughly the size of the United States, much less of its territory is suitable for agriculture. In addition, the major farming areas in the United States are located in the central part of the country, while the population is concentrated on its two coasts. But China's population is located exactly where its arable land is. As China industrializes and its cities grow ever larger, urbanization consumes what little cropland exists. This has become a problem of increasing importance in recent years.

Another feature of much of China's landscape is the scarcity of trees. Originally heavily forested, over the millennia, China has cut down its trees for fuel and to increase the amount of arable land. Soil erosion and a drier climate have resulted. The dearth of trees (and thus fuel) has influenced Chinese cooking methods: Stir-frying in a wok uses the least amount of both fuel and cooking oil.

Mountains, Rivers, and Water Control

Mountains crisscross China in all directions, in general, but China's topography rises as one moves west. The east coast plains have the lowest elevation. To the west are plateaus and finally, some of the highest mountains in the world. Four of Asia's greatest rivers originate in the high plateau and mountains of Western China: the Yellow, Yangtze (Chang Jiang), Mekong and Salween Rivers.

The first two, the Yellow and the Yangtze, are China's most important geographic features. The Yellow, which flows through North China, was the cradle of Chinese civilization. The Yangtze is navigable far into the heartland of China. Both rivers are used for transportation, communication, drinking water, and irrigation. Both originate in the same high region, and both flow east to the Pacific. Both have built up broad flood plains in the east, which have become the major agricultural areas of China. Both are subject to major flooding, particularly the Yellow River in North China. Because of the population density in the Yellow and Yangtze river valleys, flooding causes not only great loss of property and agricultural products, but also the deaths of thousands or even millions of people.

Because of such circumstances, water control has become one of the most important government functions, and to a large extent, the major criterion of an effective administration. Since ancient times, the Chinese have built dikes along the rivers to hold back flood waters. The Yellow River carries with it a great burden of fine yellow soil, hence its name. Deposits of this rich soil have formed the North China plain as, over the millennia, the great river changed its course countless times. As populations on the plain increased, the changes in the river's course caused such great economic hardship that the river became known as "China's Sorrow." Today new dikes and great dams, which cause great controversy, attempt to control the rivers.

Water control is crucial to feeding China's vast population. Given the shortage of arable land, the Chinese have traditionally practiced a type of cultivation known as intensive agriculture. Fields are small and every bit of land is used; nothing is wasted. Irrigation is used to make sure that the crops receive the proper amount of water, regardless of natural rainfall. In addition, as many crops as possible, sometimes two or three, are raised during a year, and more than one crop is sometimes planted in the same fields. In central and south China, rice is grown in special fields called paddies. Rice requires hot weather and water, so these fields are like shallow earthen pans that can be filled with water.

Because China has relatively little flatland, in order to create more fields for crops, the Chinese have learned to cut flat fields into hillsides. They turn the slope into a kind of giant stairway. Each of the "stair treads" is a flat area where farmers can raise crops. This is called *terracing*.

Climate and Lifestyle

Climate in China varies greatly from area to area, but in general the north has hot summers, cold winters, and low rainfall concentrated in the summer months. In contrast, the south has mild winters and heavy rainfall. Central and south China are suitable for wet rice cultivation, and therefore rice is the staple food. In the north, however, wheat and other grains predominate, and northerners eat foods made from wheat, such as noodles, dumplings, and steamed buns. The dividing line between the two climatic zones is the Qinling (Ch'in-ling) Mountains. This range of east-west mountains in the center of the country prevents warm, moisture-bearing winds from reaching the north in summer, and the cold, dry winds of the northern interior of Asia from reaching the south in winter.

Intensive agriculture is labor-intensive. Many people are required to prepare fields and plant, tend, and harvest crops. Working together cooperatively was necessary, whether to terrace hillsides or build and maintain dikes to control rivers. With so high a percentage of China's population inhabiting so small a part of the landmass, people must live in very close quarters. Therefore they must devise ways of living in harmony. Confucianism, China's dominant philosophy, emphasizes correct relationships between people, social order, and stability.

China is a land where natural disasters, such as floods, droughts, and earthquakes, are common. It is also a land of great geographic contrasts and/or extremes, encompassing climates from deserts to monsoon tropics. The Chinese, therefore, have also needed to learn to live with nature. Daoism (Taoism), another major philosophy of China, emphasizes harmony between people and nature. These two attitudes, the desire to live as one with nature, but also the need to manage it, lie at the heart of Chinese civilization.

Food and Cooking

A Chinese meal consists of some kind of starch, with dishes of meat and vegetables. The starch can be rice, steamed bread, noodles, "pancakes," or gruel (a thin cereal made from oats). The meat and vegetables vary, and they are mixed in various ways to combine different flavors, colors, and textures. Meat and poultry is most often used to flavor the staple food, which is rice in the east and southeast and pasta noodles north of Beijing.

Because of the scarcity of arable land, little is used for grazing cattle. Most Chinese don't have beef with their meals very often. However, they usually are able to raise animals for food that don't require much space, such as chickens, ducks, pigs, or goats.

Wood and other fuel is scarce, so the Chinese have evolved ways of preparing and cooking food to save fuel. Food is cut into small pieces, which increases the surface area and decreases the thickness, so the food is cooked quickly. The way foods are cooked saves fuel too. Stir-frying is the most common: The cut-up meat and vegetables are cooked on high heat with a small amount of oil, in a *wok*, a rounded frying pan. The cook can rotate the food up the sides of the pan so it cooks rapidly but doesn't burn. Other cooking techniques include: deep frying, steaming, boiling, stewing, and smoking. Baking is not often done at home because it uses too much fuel.

Eating Etiquette

In China, the most important thing is to enjoy eating, but certain rules should be followed. The table is usually set with a small bowl, chopsticks, a porcelain spoon, and a small dish. Food is served in large serving dishes which are placed in the center of the table. Generally, a serving spoon, or serving chopsticks is in the dish. Otherwise, you use your own porcelain spoon or chopsticks to help yourself. The rule is that you must eat what you touch. If there are guests, the host sits closest to the door and the most important guest farthest from it, with others arranged between them. Younger people sit closer to the host. No one leaves until the guest of honor retires from the table. Generally, you will not eat too much at the beginning of the meal, and as each course is cleared you will only take as much as you can eat in later courses. First, there will be a cold hors d'oeuvre and then the hot dishes. The best dishes come first, followed by lesser or secondary dishes. You don't need to take food you don't like, but it is bad manners to take food and not eat it. Tea is always served with dinner. At the end of the meal, soup is served to clear the palate, followed by fruit or sweets. A full-course meal for guests might include ten dishes. At a family dinner, soup and four dishes are enough, balancing meat, fish, eggs, and vegetables, lightly and heavily seasoned dishes, and foods prepared using different cooking methods.

Activity #1

Learning with Maps

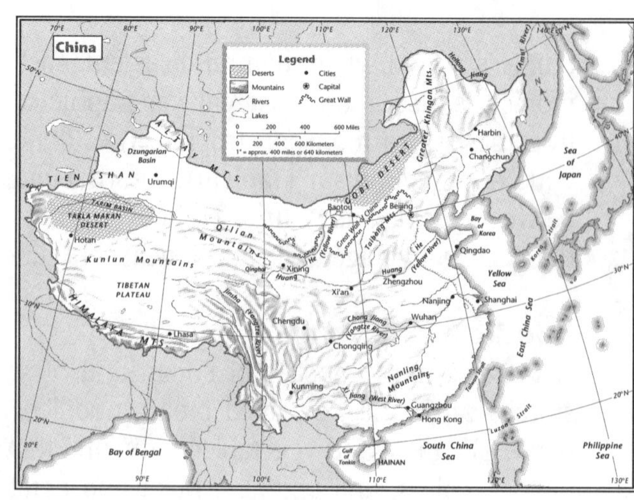

Overview

Working with a number of special purpose maps, students make observations that help them to answer questions of increasing difficulty—from reading material directly from maps to making inferences using several maps at once.

Goals

1. Students review and strengthen map skills.
2. Students become familiar with the geographical features of China.
3. Students understand the relationship between geography and lifestyle.

Materials

Duplicate sets of maps: China; Major Rivers, Mountains & Deserts; Surrounding Nations; Population Density; Agricultural Regions. (Pages 21-25)

If possible, reproduce the maps on *transparencies for copiers* (Ordinary acetate transparencies will melt in the copy machine.) and display on an overhead projector. We recommend that 2-3 students work together, with one set of maps for each team. We collect ours and store them in pocket folders for reuse.

Procedure

1. Compose a list of questions that may be answered by looking at *one map*. Ask teams to write the name of the map they used *and* the answer to the question. For example:

- Which country is north of central China? (Surrounding Nations: Outer Mongolia)
- Name 3 cities in China. (China: Hong Kong, Hotan, Shanghai)
- What is the capital of China? (China: Bejing)
- List the mountain ranges in China. (Major Rivers, Mountains & Deserts: Quinling, Nanling, Talhang, Himalya, Kunlun, Tian Shan, and Altai)
- What is the longest river in China? (Major Rivers, Mountains & Deserts: Yangtse River)

2. Compose a second list of questions that may be answered by looking at *two maps*. Ask teams to write the names of the two maps they used and the answer to the question. For example:

- What rivers run through the most heavily cultivated areas? (Major Rivers, Mountains & Deserts and Agricultural Regions: Yellow and Yangstze)
- What cities are in the most heavily populated parts of China? (China and Population Density: Bejing and Shanghai)
- What geographic feature separates China from Nepal? (Surrounding Nations and Major Rivers, Mountains & Deserts: Himalaya's)
- What rivers form part of the border between China and Russia? (Surrounding Nations and Major Rivers, Mountains & Deserts: Amur)

3. Allow time for a group discussion on the more interesting or challenging questions.

4. Distribute cpoies of the Surrounding Nations map (page 23) to each student. On the chalkboard, start a list called "Important Features of China." Solicit suggestions. Ask the students to justify their responses. Add to the list yourself if you need to. Then, using the map packet, have students make their own maps, incorporating features from a variety of maps, while guided by the list on the board.

Teaching Strategies

Things to decide based on your students:

1. How many questions should be in each section? Should all the students have the same number of questions of each type?

2. In what form should the questions be presented? A chart on a worksheet? Written on the chalkboard?

5. As a final challange, ask each team to use the maps to discover why China began in the region it did and why that region flourished.

6. Have students compose original questions using one or more maps. Use the questions in a class game.

ACTIVITY #2
Making a China Relief Map

Overview
Students will work in pairs or trios on desktop maps of China. All the groups might make the same maps, with major geographical features, or small groups might make special purpose maps emphasizing aspects such as river systems or climate.

Goals
1. Students review and strengthen map skills.
2. Students go from a two- to a three-dimensional medium to reinforce geographical information.
3. Students appreciate the variety of natural features of China.

Materials
Map sets (pages 21–25) and any other maps that show relief/topography; 3/8" plywood, cut to approximately 9" x 12" (if this is not available, corrugated cardboard will do); wheat paste or wallpaper paste; tempera paints, brushes; sawdust (if your school doesn't have a wood shop or a cooperative custodian, try the local lumberyard.) You can also use quick-drying clay for this activity.

Procedure
1. Students should trace the outline of China onto the plywood.

2. Mix the wallpaper paste in a large bucket according to directions.

3. Dole out a cup or two of plaster at a time. To that amount, add sufficient sawdust to make a paste wet enough to be sticky, but dry enough to be molded like clay.

4. Using their maps as guides, students will build up mountain ranges and deserts, river systems and plains. Generally, the topography will get higher from east to west.

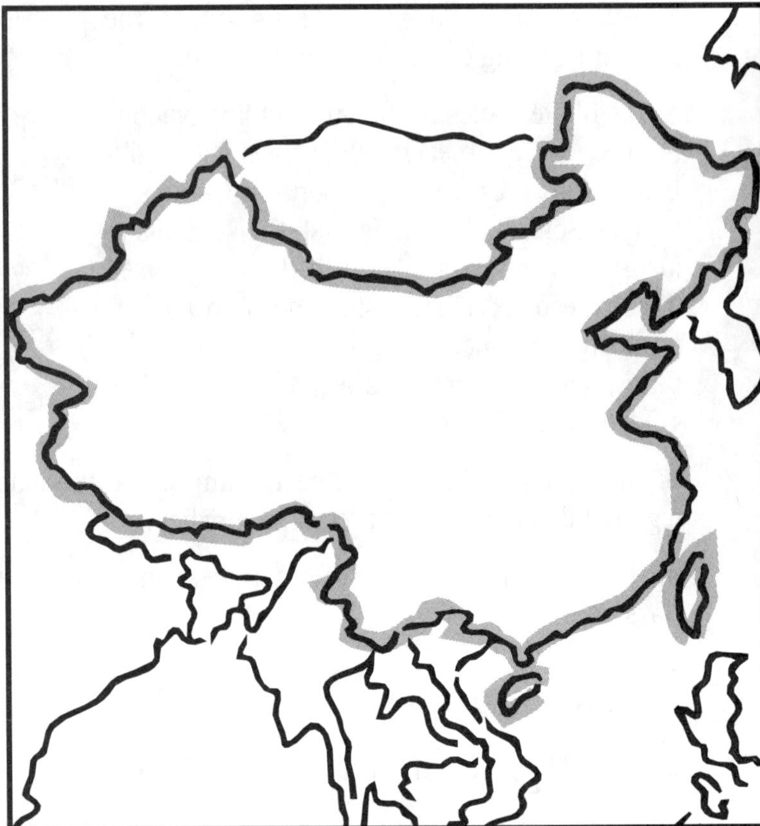

5. The models will usually dry overnight, after which they may be painted. One possibility is that they be painted green, yellow, orange, and brown as features rise above sea level. Students could then make a key indicating elevation. Since elevation may change radically between similar features (like deserts), you may also direct students to label their maps.

6. Discuss what students noticed as a result of making a map that they hadn't noticed just looking at one. Ask whether they think they will remember the map better and if so, why this is. Discuss what is was like to work in this medium. What were problems encountered? Did it get easier as students went along? What techniques did people invent to make it work better?

7. Solicit questions from students that are based on what they've learned or observed during this activity. Think about how some of the questions might be addressed in future activities.

8. Display the maps.

Teaching Strategies

1. **Make a Bigger Map:** More mature thinkers might be able to scale up a smaller map into a larger one: Talk about what scale is. Project a map transparency on a screen. Move the projector back and ask students to tell you what happens to the map. Discuss what happens to the scale of distance as the map increases in size. Then challenge groups of students to make relief maps that are scaled up perhaps twice the size of their guide maps.

2. **Going Beyond Borders:** The topography continues beyond China's borders. Often children looking at the map of a single country are misled when surrounding geography is not shown. One way to deal with this is to instruct students to extend natural features to the edge of their maps and to color the areas that are outside China gray or some other neutral color.

ACTIVITY #3

Crossing China by Sampan

Overview

Students will discover how China's topography impedes travel and communication in all but one part of the country, the East, by *sailing* and *portaging* a sampan, a traditional flat bottomed boat, between different points.

Materials

Map 1: China, and Map 2: Major Rivers, Mountains & Deserts (pages 21 and 22)

Procedure

1. All the groups will begin in Harbin, in the northeast corner. Then, each will go to one of the following:

- Route 1: to Hainan Island
- Route 2: Lhasa
- Route 3: Kunming (in South China)
- Route 4: Urumqi (in Western China)

2. Some directions to students:

- Each group will want to stay in the water as much as possible, because crossing land means having to portage, or carry, your sampan.
- Each time you have gone as far as you can using a water route, write down the name of the body of water and the distance you traveled. Write "U" if you are traveling upstream and "D" if you are traveling downstream.
- Each time you travel on land, write the number of miles you portage before you encounter water again. If you have to cross a dessert, a mountain, or any other geographical feature, record that information too.
- Have individuals in the group take turns navigating and recording.

3. Debrief the class. Allow each group to report about their attempts to get to their destinations. Ask them in which part of China was travel by sampan easiest? Most difficult? Why? Ask them what consequences this may have had on how China developed throughout history. (Water travel facilitates communication and commerce. The parts of China that have been connected by water throughout the centuries are the most developed. The western regions are mountainous or deserts, features that are barriers to progress.)

> *Teaching Strategy*
>
> **Graphic Organizer:** You might want to make a chart to facilitate the recording of information; include place of origin, alternating spaces for rivers and portaging, number of miles, U or D, and destination.

Follow-up Activities

Current Events: Read current articles on construction of the Three Gorges Dam on the Yangtze River. Have a debate on whether the Chinese should construct the dam. Discuss similarities between the problems posed by the Yangtze River and those of rivers in the United States which flood. A research spin-off would be to investigate dam building in the United States, such as the Hoover Dam.

ACTIVITY #4
Geography and Cooking

Overview

Students should be able to make the connection between the kinds of foods the Chinese eat and the style in which they are prepared, and the geography of China. At the same time, they will develop and practice getting and giving directions.

For the geography connection, prepare two dishes: fried noodles (North China) and fried rice (South China). Discuss with students why each dish is typical of that region of China.

Michael B 422
Fried rice
Ingredients
serves a large group
2 pieces of ginger
2 Leeks
2 eggs
4 tablespoons [illegible]
bowl of rice

To develop and practice getting and giving directions, explain to the group that you are going to demonstrate how to make a typical Chinese dish. They should take notes on what you say and do, because you will ask them to write a recipe for the dish later, and they won't get any printed information about it.

Materials

Wok or large frying pan, Chinese scoop or spatula, stove or electric hot plate, cutting boards (you can improvise), knives, bowls or plates, chopsticks.

Recipe

For recipies, try the following cookbooks: *Chinese Cooking: an Illustrated Guide* (Barons, 1981) and *Joyce Chen Cook Book* (Lippincott, 1962). We often substitute egg for meat as it costs less and suits almost everyone's dietary restrictions. Spaghetti (not too thin) is a fine substitute for real Chinese noodles.

Tips on Cooking with Students

You need to observe certain guidelines for this to be successful. First, cook in small groups—not more than half a class at a time. Then break that half group down to smaller groups for certain jobs. Second, have a task for every student, even if you have to divide a task between two of them. Third, have enough equipment on hand to get the job done without waiting. Fourth, allow students time to eat what they have prepared. Fifth, make sure that cleanup is part of the process.

Map 1.

Name ______________________

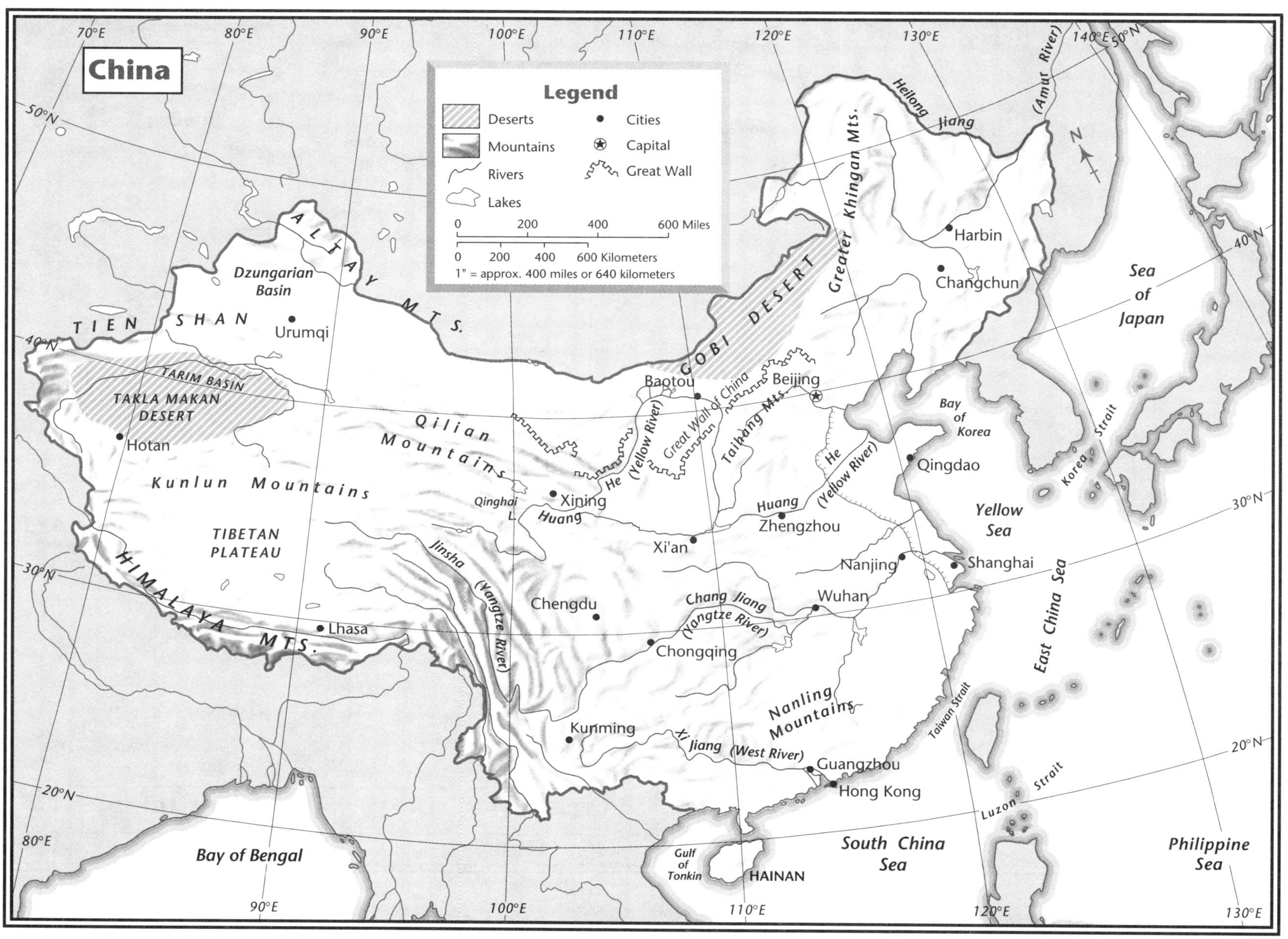
China
Legend
Deserts
Mountains
Rivers
Lakes
Cities
Capital
Great Wall
0 200 400 600 Miles
0 200 400 600 Kilometers
1" = approx. 400 miles or 640 kilometers
ALTAY MTS.
TIEN SHAN
Dzungarian Basin
Urumqi
TARIM BASIN
TAKLA MAKAN DESERT
Hotan
Kunlun Mountains
Qilian Mountains
TIBETAN PLATEAU
HIMALAYA MTS.
Lhasa
Qinghai L.
Xining
Huang
He (Yellow River)
Great Wall of China
Baotou
GOBI DESERT
Greater Khingan Mts.
Heilong Jiang
(Amur River)
Harbin
Changchun
Beijing
Taihang Mts.
Bay of Korea
Qingdao
Huang He (Yellow River)
Zhengzhou
Xi'an
Jinsha (Yangtze River)
Chengdu
Chongqing
Chang Jiang (Yangtze River)
Wuhan
Nanjing
Shanghai
Kunming
Nanling Mountains
Xi Jiang (West River)
Guangzhou
Hong Kong
Gulf of Tonkin
HAINAN
Bay of Bengal
South China Sea
Yellow Sea
East China Sea
Sea of Japan
Korea Strait
Taiwan Strait
Luzon Strait
Philippine Sea
N
70°E
80°E
90°E
100°E
110°E
120°E
130°E
140°E
50°N
40°N
30°N
20°N

Map 2.

Name ____________________

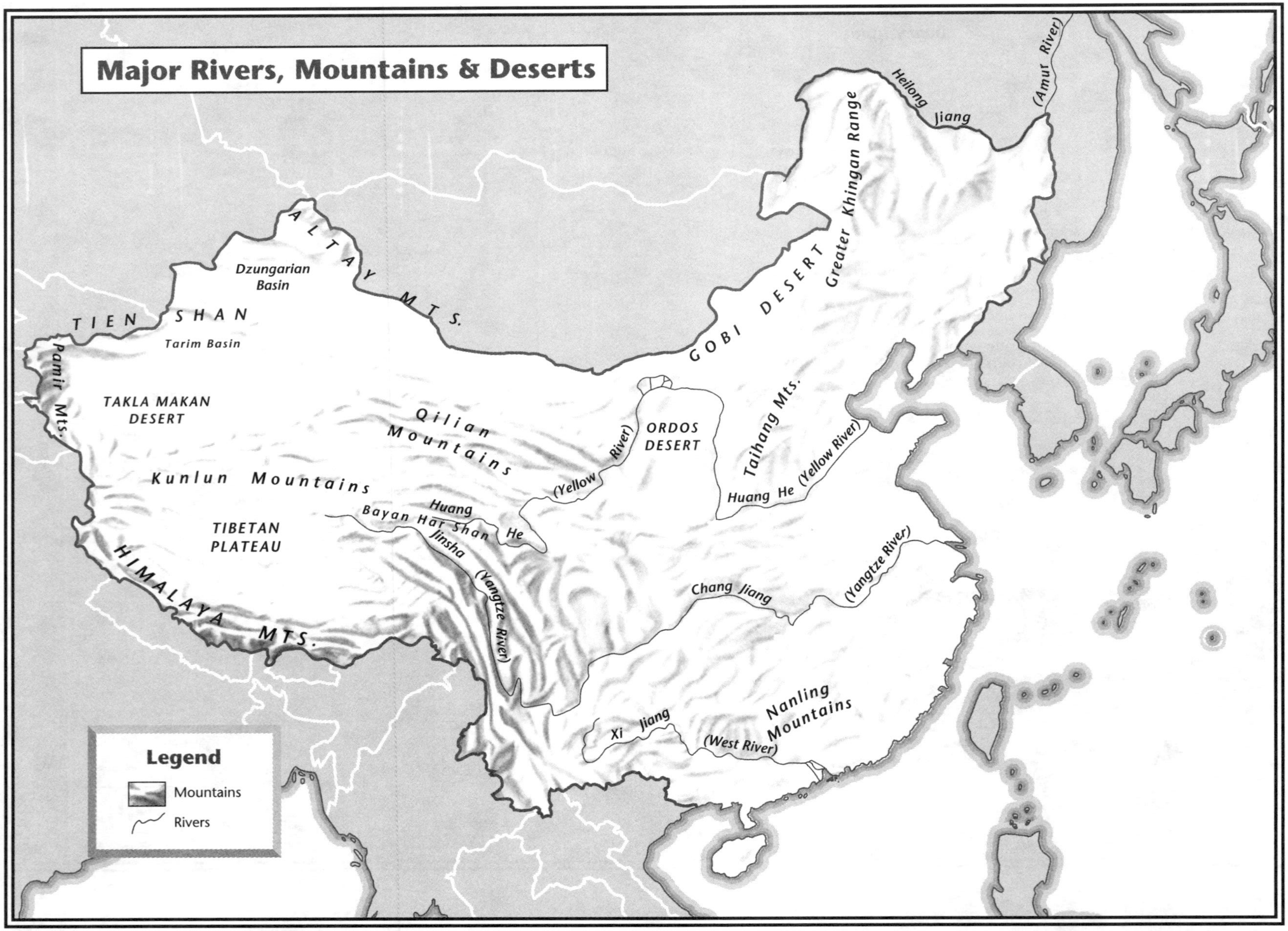

Major Rivers, Mountains & Deserts
Heilong Jiang
(Amur River)
Greater Khingan Range
ALTAY MTS.
Dzungarian Basin
GOBI DESERT
TIEN SHAN
Tarim Basin
Pamir Mts.
TAKLA MAKAN DESERT
Qilian Mountains
Taihang Mts.
ORDOS DESERT
(Yellow River)
Huang He (Yellow River)
Kunlun Mountains
Huang He
Bayan Har Shan
Jinsha (Yangtze River)
TIBETAN PLATEAU
HIMALAYA MTS.
Chang Jiang (Yangtze River)
Xi Jiang (West River)
Nanling Mountains
Legend
Mountains
Rivers

Map 3.

Name ______________________________

Surrounding Nations
RUSSIA
KAZAKHSTAN
MONGOLIA
KYRGYZSTAN
TAJIKISTAN
AFGHANISTAN
PAKISTAN
CHINA
NORTH KOREA
SOUTH KOREA
JAPAN
NEPAL
BHUTAN
INDIA
INDIA
BANGLADESH
MYANMAR (BURMA)
VIETNAM
LAOS
THAILAND
TAIWAN
PHILIPPINES

Map 4.

Name ______________________________

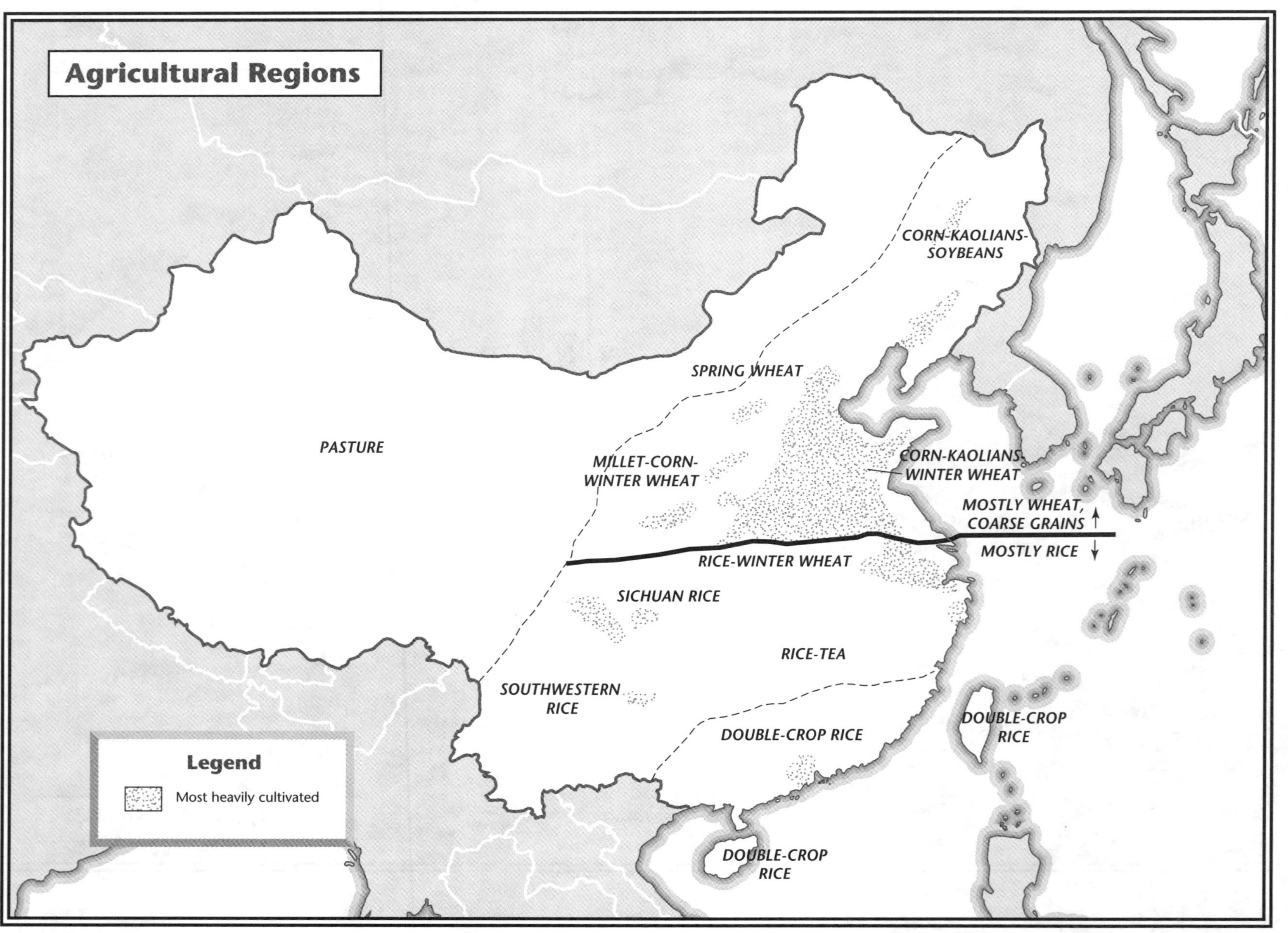
Agricultural Regions
PASTURE
SPRING WHEAT
CORN-KAOLIANS-SOYBEANS
MILLET-CORN-WINTER WHEAT
CORN-KAOLIANS-WINTER WHEAT
MOSTLY WHEAT, COARSE GRAINS
MOSTLY RICE
RICE-WINTER WHEAT
SICHUAN RICE
RICE-TEA
SOUTHWESTERN RICE
DOUBLE-CROP RICE
DOUBLE-CROP RICE
DOUBLE-CROP RICE
Legend
Most heavily cultivated

Map 5.

Name ____________________

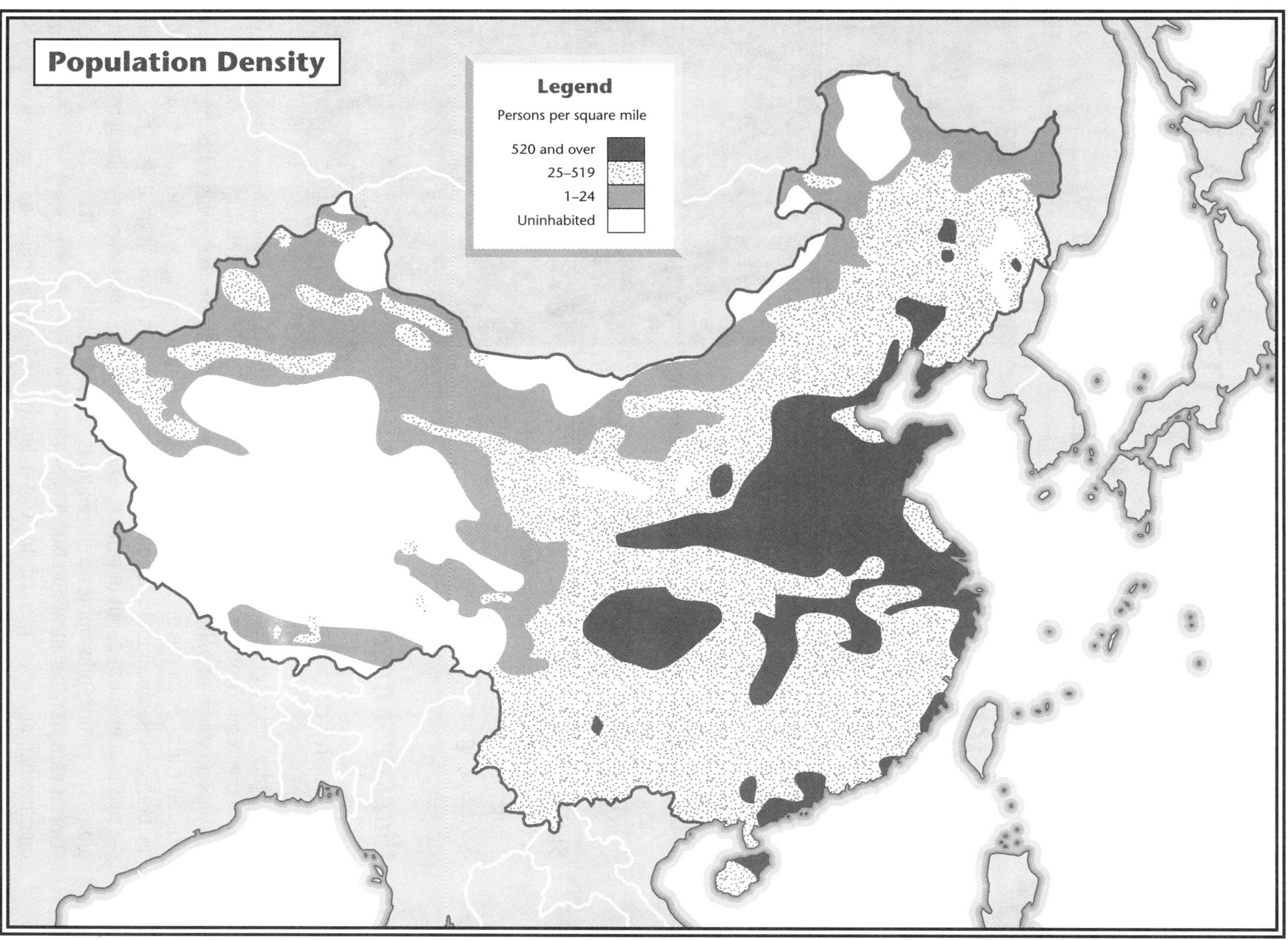
Population Density
Legend
Persons per square mile
520 and over
25–519
1–24
Uninhabited

CHAPTER 2

PHILOSOPHY AND RELIGION

Goals for the Unit

Concepts

1. Philosophy and religion are systems for guiding one's beliefs, values, and actions.
2. Chinese philosophies affected ideas of how the society should be ordered, and the way in which Chinese people regarded and interacted with people from outside of China.
3. The major philosophies of ancient China have affected the attitudes and behavior of Chinese up to the present.
4. Belief systems influence many parts of a culture.

Skills

1. Comparing and organizing different views.
2. Interpreting allegory.
3. Analyzing world views.

Background Information

Philosophy and Religion in China

Philosophy, a system for living one's life, and religion, the belief in a superhuman power whom one respects or worships, are guiding principles in human history. If we think of philosophy as a system of values to live by, as the part of religion that deals with the way you act here on earth, or as the guideline for what is right and wrong, we can understand that there are both philosophical and religious aspects to systems of thought. In China, the line between the two is often blurred, but in general, Chinese are more interested in philosophy than in religion. The main philosophies and religions of traditional China have been Confucianism, Daoism (Taoism), Legalism and Buddhism. These four schools of thought often complemented one another, and even merged. In Asia, religions and philosophies do not demand exclusive adherents; rather, a person can believe in several simultaneously.

Traditional Philosophies

Confucianism

Confucius, the Latin version of the Chinese "Kong Fuzi" (K'ung Fu-tzu) or Master Kong, was a teacher who lived from 551-479 B.C. This was a time of devastating civil warfare and social unrest in China, so it is understandable that Confucius's goal was to create a peaceful, stable society. His ideas formed a social philosophy that focused on the importance of how people relate to one another. Some of his basic ideas were that education overcomes ignorance and lack of harmony, that people are good, and that they live in a network of social and political relationships. The ideal ruler is an educated, moral person who guides society through the example of his own good conduct.

Confucius stressed five relationships as key to a stable, harmonious society: ruler to subject, father to son, husband to wife, older brother to younger brother, and friend to friend. The first four relationships are unequal; the first person is superior to the second. The fifth, friendship, however, is equal and should be based on love and mutual respect. If we remember the unsettled times in which he lived, Confucius' emphasis on high ethical standards and correct relationships becomes very understandable. Duty, combined with sincerity, was the path to harmony.

Confucius thought of himself as preserving the old ways which had been lost during troubled times. Yet, in fact, he introduced a whole new way of looking at society. The fundamental principle in his ideas is that only virtue gives one the right to rule, not heredity. Furthermore, virtue could be acquired through education. These ideas were very different from those which had existed up until then.

Daoism

Daoism is a philosophy rooted in the idea that the "dao" or way is the principle by which everything works, the life force of all natural things. The place of people in the universe is really insignificant. Daoists are against all organizations, including formal education. Their goal is to create a society in harmony with the world, which can be achieved if people follow the dao. Daoists believe in nonaction, not interfering in the affairs of others, both on the part of individuals and states. Because they consider ambition and desire to be the causes of social unrest, they stress simplicity, humility, quiet, plainness, and peace. To epitomize the power of the "dao," they use the symbol of water: Water seems weak, always seeks the easiest way, always flows downhill, yet will wear away stone.

While Confucianism forms an idealistic way of thinking about governing, Daoism rejects government altogether. For Daoists, the ideal ruler is one who does not govern. Daoism became the counterbalance to Confucianism. Daoism stressed harmony with nature, while Confucianism stressed harmony between people. Throughout the millennia, the Chinese have found that something of each philosophy answered their own needs.

Legalism

The third determining idea of Chinese thinking was Legalism. Its followers believed that people are motivated by greed and fear, and that a well-defined system of punishment and reward is necessary to control their behavior. Rewards were given to those who obeyed the state, punishments to those who did not. Severe punishments such as the death penalty, were necessary to prevent undesirable behavior. Furthermore, people were required to report any infringement of the laws, or to be considered culpable themselves. However, they were supposed to report good as well as bad behavior. The basic idea of the Legalists was that there was, in fact, no absolute right or wrong. Laws replaced morality as guidelines of behavior.

Legalists believed that government should be based on the world as it actually exists. They rejected both the supernatural and tradition. They believed that a good ruler maintains and, if possible, expands the state's borders. A ruler governs using laws, rewards and punishments.

Legalism was the professed philosophy of government of the First Emperor of China (Qin Shi Huangdi). However, his ruthless persecution of Confucian scholars and texts gave legalism a bad name. Many Chinese rulers have followed its tenets, but without acknowledging it. Students of modern totalitarian political systems will see similarities, and understand its appeal as a practical guide to controlling a population. Nevertheless, the legalist doctrine itself remained a covert view of government.

Buddhism

Buddhism, the most recent system to spread over China, was introduced from India in the first century A.D. Buddhism is the only major Chinese philosophy which is not concerned with governing, but rather with individual behavior. Buddhism actually controlled all aspects of daily life. A Buddhist does not eat meat, does not kill, believes in rebirth, and believes that how a person lives affects his or her future existences.

According to Buddhist teachings, there is a universal spirit of which every living thing is a part. A person experiences continuous re-birth or reincarnations, until he or she reaches a state of enlightenment—or the realization that worldly desires and attachments are an illusion causing only suffering. However, one's fate can be controlled by human efforts. A person who practices good moral conduct, discipline, and meditation moves upward through successive existences to an ultimate reward, "nirvana," or nonexistence, ending the chain of painful rebirths.

Traditional Religions

Ancient beliefs

The ancient beliefs of China pre-date any of the above philosophies, and have influenced the Chinese over the centuries. The most important belief is ancestor "worship." The Chinese believe that the souls of dead people live on as spirits, which in turn can advise and influence their descendants. There are actually two souls. One is buried with the body, and requires offerings to keep it there; the other leaves the body at the time of death, but it, too, requires offerings to keep it happy.

In addition to the souls of departed ancestors, the Chinese believed in many nature gods, who needed to be appeased. Polytheism gradually incorporated aspects of Daoism and Buddhism, resulting in amalgamations of belief often referred to as folk Daoism and folk Buddhism.

Folk Daoism and Folk Buddhism

Both Daoism and Buddhism have popular religious followings and accommodated many manifestations of the Dao and Buddha, even borrowing from each other. Buddhism, as it spread throughout China, began to bear little resemblance to the original philosophy. Nirvana became heaven, and salvation was possible through faith and prayer. An array of Boddhisattvas, those who had reached enlightenment but stayed to help others, were there to provide hope and solace for ordinary people. Buddhism gave to Daoism the idea of reincarnation. Daoism developed a pantheon which mirrored the imperial bureaucracy in heaven and hell, with the Jade Emperor as the head, and demons and ghosts bullying the damned.

Islam

Islam is an important religion in China, particularly among the Hui minority in Xinjiang. However, China's 35 million Muslims are both Han Chinese, and Chinese citizens of Turkic origin. Introduced into China in the Tang Dynasty, the religion was most popular during the Song and Yuan Dynasties, but suffered persecution under the Qing. Today, there are mosques for practicing Muslims throughout the country, but the area most Islamic in culture is the Northwest.

Christianity

Christianity was also introduced into China during the eclectic Tang Dynasty. Jesuit missionaries, such as Matteo Ricci, who came in the late 16th century, impressed the Imperial Court with their scientific knowledge. But Ricci's idea to convert the China's educated classes was undermined by infighting among the Christian orders, and Christians were marginalized until the mid-century. At that time, China's humiliating defeats by European powers forced the opening of China to Christian missionary efforts. There are a few million Christians in China today.

Talking About:
Research with Middle School Children

Millions of us have labored through research papers despite the fact that only a fraction of us will ever write a research paper after we leave school. Howard Gardner said, "We subject everyone to an education where, if you succeed, you will be best suited to be a college professor." Was he talking in part about writing research papers? Should we teachers abandon the project because it's not "authentic" for most Americans?

Important Skills

It's not important for students to scramble around to deliver dull and imitative papers. It is important to consider the scores of skills that are imbedded in this process.

Among the thinking skills essential even for noncollege professors are the following: comparing, summarizing, observing, interpreting, criticizing, looking for assumptions, imagining, hypothesizing, decision making, applying facts and principles to new situations, and formulating questions or problems.

There are, in addition to research and writing, skills in gathering, organizing, and presenting information: locating resources, using a table of contents and an index, skimming, recognizing main ideas, taking notes, identifying sources, ordering ideas, making an outline, using evidence, and writing paragraphs. And then there are study skills like planning and budgeting time and managing books and materials.

All in all, what a good research project can provide is a model for how an individual or group can investigate something in which there is an interest or for which there is a need. Teaching children how to do research is teaching a life skill.

We sometimes model a class project before going to a group or individual research project: In his immigration unit, Stan leads the whole class in a project about Chinese immigration. After that, groups of students do projects about other 19th-century immigrant groups (e.g., Italian, Japanese, Mexican). Finally, each individual does a research project on a contemporary immigrant in his or her community. The procedure and aspects of the three projects are the same, so students develop both competence and confidence.

Jigsawing and Reassembling

There has been debate about the effectiveness of jigsawing, that is, taking a topic for research and cutting it into parts for which different students or groups are responsible. The problem is that students develop expertise on their section, but may not get a sense of the whole. To help students assemble the pieces, we've used different strategies: First, when students present the results of their research, we ask them to write five key questions on the chalkboard that will be answered in their reports. Listeners are required to take notes on the answers. This information becomes part of the material for which everyone is responsible.

Another way to deal with jigsawing is to break students up into groups, so each group develops expertise in an aspect of a topic. Within the group, students talk with each other and check each others' information and thinking. Then reorganize the class into mixed groups containing an expert from each of the first groups. Each expert is then interviewed by the others.

Another variation is to have the students record their research (in reports, fact sheets, models, pictures, maps, timelines, etc.) and have each set up a station that includes a list of important questions that may be answered by examining the materials there. Students rotate from one to the next and then find and write the answers to the questions for themselves.

It Doesn't Have to Be a Paper

There are many methods of presenting information. The dynasty research project in the History chapter directs groups of children to record their research on a large illustrated timeline. Both of us have the groups make HyperStudio presentations about their dynasties, and before we had that technology, students made scrapbooks.

But It Might Be a Paper

There are times when our students write research papers even if these are not always as interesting as other forms of presentation. One benefit of a paper is that it is portable and postable (on bulletin boards and websites). It can be read by a large number of people. Students may grumble about sharing, but most of them are pleased when a reader comments on their work. And while our students may communicate as adults using sounds and images, audio and video, writing clearly will remain an essential, useful life skill.

Activity #1

Using a Graphic Organizer to Take Notes

Overview

Students learn about the major philosophies and religions in China.

Goals

1. Students compare the underlying ideas of the different philosophies of China.

2. Students organize that comparison in a visual form.

Material

- Graphic Organizer: Comparing Philosophies reproducible (page 36)
- Background Information: Philosophy and Religion in China (pages 26-29)

Name Louis Patino

Graphic Organizer: *Comparing Philosophies*

Categories	Confucianism	Daoism	Legalism	Buddhism
Ways of looking at life	Focuses on the importance of how people relate to one another.			
Basic ideas	• People are good • People need education to overcome ignorance			
Goals	• To create a peaceful and stable society			
Ideal leader	• an educated moral person who guides society through his good conduct			

CHINA SCHOLASTIC PROFESSIONAL BOOKS 36

Procedure

1. Read and discuss the passage on Confucianism. Use topics listed on the graphic organizer to guide your discussion. Invite students to fill in each of the boxes under Confucianism.

2. Students can then fill in the boxes as they learn about the other philosophies.

Option 1: If students need more help with this task, fill in the section on Confucianism on the graphic organizer for students to use as a model.

Option 2: If your students are able to think more abstractly, you might ask the class what questions are answered by the passage. Guide them to look at topic sentences in paragraphs. Then use their questions to investigate the other three philosophies, using a grid such as the one provided.

3. Now use their data to discuss the following:

- With the exception of Buddhism, the major philosophies of traditional China were all set forth as ideas for governing the state. Which philosophies, or parts of philosophies, might have worked? Which might have been impractical for governing?
- Which philosophies might work in our country today? Which would not work? Explain.
- Think about the lifestyle of most Americans. Which aspects of our lifestyle would be consistent or inconsistent with each of the philosophies? One way to explore this is to present a situation and ask how a person who is an adherent of each of the four philosophies would respond to it. For example:

  You are in a flower shop and accidentally knock over a vase. The vase breaks and the flowers are destroyed. What is your reaction? What is the reaction of the shopkeeper? What is the reaction of the government (the law)?

  You find a winning lottery ticket; if you keep it, you will be fabulously wealthy. What is your reaction? What is the reaction of the person who lost it? Your friends and family? What is the reaction of the government?

Follow-up Activities

Venn Diagram: On a sheet of chart paper, make two large intersecting circles, each about a foot in diameter. Label one "Confucianism" and the other "Buddhism." Challenge the class to think about which beliefs are characteristic of one philosophy but not the other, and which characteristics both share. Write the beliefs in the appropriate spaces on the diagram. This diagram can be used to compare and contrast any two philosophies. (We've tried three intersecting circles as well but, frankly, it obscured as much as it clarified.)

Confucianism, Legalism, and Communism: Later on, when you discuss the ideologies of modern China, revisit the philosophies of Confucianism and Legalism. Both can be compared with Communism. (See Chapter 7: Modern China for an information chart.)

Activity #2
The Analects of Confucius

Overview

Though Confucius played an essential role in the shaping of China's history, relatively little is known about him. What Confucius really said are known as the Analects, which means *conversations.* Much of The Analects consist of sayings of the Master (Confucius) in response to his students questions.

Goals

1. Students become familiar with some of the ideas of Confucius.
2. Students think about some of the attitudes and beliefs which inform their own behavior.

Materials

- Selections from the Analects of Confucius reproducible (page 37).
- Construction paper and other materials to make posters (markers, rulers, pencils, etc.).

Procedure

1. Share with the class the information about Confucius provided on page 27. (For more information on Confucius, see the Resources section for Web sites.) You might use the information in the reading provided.

2. Hand out copies of the Analects of Confucius reproducible to students or make a transparency and project them for the class to see.

3. Give students time to read and to try to make sense of them. Explain to students that in many translations of the Analects, Confucius begins with the expression "The superior man...." Discuss with the class why he did so. Why are women not mentioned? What might he have meant by "superior"?

4. Ask students to select three analects they feel are interesting and still relevant. Have them copy the three analects onto writing paper. Then have students paraphrase each analect and give a brief example (a real-life situation) of how it might be relevant to our present-day lives.

5. Invite students to share their choices and their interpretations of them.

6. Have students make posters of one of the analects. The analect is written across the bottom

Teaching Strategies

1. Interpreting Figurative Language: While some students might have slightly different spins on some of the analects, there will be interpretations that are just wrong. We've developed a number of respectful ways to tell students that that they're wrong and let them know it's fine to make mistakes. To establish a safe classroom where students will take risks and share their responses even if they aren't sure, we teach students ways to introduce responses they aren't positive about. Also, we can enforce a no-laughing policy from the outset: When people make mistakes or have accidents, don't laugh, even if you feel like it. And then, see what you can do to help the situation.

2. The Think-Aloud Strategy: Here's a strategy that's helpful not only to interpret unfamiliar syntax or poetry, but even ordinary text: Model a technique of reading aloud in which you pause after each chunk of meaning and paraphrase that piece (or ask your students what it means). As you continue, go back to the beginning of the sentence and join the paraphrased chunks together, until you have restated the whole sentence in your/their own words. Then, later, even when students can't paraphrase a chunk on their own, they can often identify the part of the sentence that blocks them from understanding the meaning of the whole thing.

or the paper. Then students illustrate its wisdom (either representationally or abstractly). Display students' posters around the classroom.

Follow-up Activities

Original Wisdom: Ask students to compose analects of their own, trying to imitate the syntax and tone of Confucius's analects. Discuss the values that underlie these sayings. Then type up and reproduce all the original analects for distribution to the class. Ask students to make a poster of someone else's analect.

Poor Richard and Mao: There are similarities between Benjamin Franklin's aphorisms in *Poor Richard's Almanack* and the Analects. Both writings are brief, proverbial, and encourage great personal responsiblity. There are any number of activities students could engage in by using passages from both. Note that while Mao Zedong sought to eradicate all traces of traditional Chinese thought, his *Quotations from Chairman Mao*, the "Little Red Book," is actually similar in form to the Analects. Later in the study, the Analects might be revisited and compared to the Quotations.

Activity #3

Daoism

Overview

Daoism is particularly appealing to young people because of its ideal of harmony with nature, its anarchistic view of organization and authority, and its emphasis on peace and simplicity. In addition, the poetry of the main Daoist text, the Tao Te Ching, is beautiful, accessible and thought-provoking, especially in the translation recommended below.

Goals

1. Students learn about the philosophy of Daoism.
2. Students interpret passages from the Tao Te Ching.

Materials:

- Copies of Selections from the Tao Te Ching (page 38)
- The Tao Te Ching, translation by Kwok, Man-Ho, Martin Palmer, and Jay Ramsey (Barnes & Noble, 1993). Alternately, the entire Tao Te Ching is available at this Web site: http://eawc.evansville.edu/anthology/tao.htm. Chapters 11, 14, 16, 22, and 48 are particularly appealing, and provide examples of the major tenets of Daoism.

Procedure

1. Reproduce copies of page 38 or make a transparency of the page and project for the students to read.

2. Give students time to read the poems from the Tao Te Ching and to make sense of them. Discuss their interpretations.

3. Invite students to read additional selections from the Tao Te Ching and select their favorites. Students can then copy and illustrate the selections and share with the class.

Follow-up Activities

Buddhism and Daoism in American Song Lyrics: You can download lyrics to almost any song at www.lyrics.ch, a searchable database. Get the lyrics for "I Got Plenty of Nothin," "The Best Things in Life Are Free," "Material Girl," "Money," and any other songs you think of that deal with the issues of wealth and happiness. It's best to play the songs for your class if you can locate recordings. Discuss the relationship between the lyrics and the ideas of Buddhism and Daoism.

Skills Practice: One of the great boons of word processing is the ease with which we can revise our writing. But we can just as easily reverse the process to give students practice in the skills that are part of our language arts curriculum. Many of our student readings are saved for reuse later. Sometimes we'll retrieve a file and put errors in it of various types (e.g., capitalization, run-ons, spelling). We double space it, print it, and distribute it. We keep a class set of red pens—our students seem to love to correct us in that color. In this way, we kill the proverbial two birds: content and skills. In addition, since the students are reading more carefully to catch all our errors, they often absorb more of the details.

ACTIVITY #4
Making Tomb Objects

Overview

The ancient beliefs and rituals of China provide opportunities to compare cultural mores of different societies and to discuss students' values today.

Materials

- Pictures of tomb figures from any Chinese art book, such as *Chinese Tomb Figurines* by Ann Paludon (Oxford University Press, 1994)
- Clay, paint, and kiln for firing, or colored plasticene

Procedure

1. Discuss with students various religious practices when a person dies. If students have studied other cultures, encourage them to tell what they know of burial customs among Native Americans, Egyptians, Mayans, etc.

2. Explain to students that in ancient China, models of people, animals, and property were buried with a person to accompany that person in the afterworld. (For more on tomb figures, see Chapter 5: Painting and Other Art.)

3. Have students discuss and decide for themselves what objects or animals are of value to them, and which they would like to take with them to a physical afterlife, if such a place existed. Students have to provide a reason for whatever they choose. Then have them make sculptures of these objects with modeling clay to put on display.

Name ____

Graphic Organizer: *Comparing Philosophies*

Categories	Confucianism	Daoism	Legalism	Buddhism
Ways of looking at life				
Basic ideas				
Goals				
Ideal leader				

Name ____

Selections from: *The Analects of Confucius*

On Family:

1. A young man's duty is to behave well to his parents at home and to his elders abroad.

2. When his father and mother are alive, a good son does not wander far away; or if he does so, goes only where he has said he was going.

On Religion:

1. Till you have learned to serve men, how can you serve ghosts?...Till you know about the living, how are you to know about the dead?

2. Wealth and rank are what every man desires, but if you can only have them by disregarding your beliefs, you must give them up. Poverty and obscurity are what every man hates, but if they can only be avoided by disregarding your beliefs, you must accept them.

On Ethics:

1. The good man does not grieve that other people do not recognize his merits. His only anxiety is that he might fail to recognize the merits of others.

2. It is only the very wisest or the very stupidest who cannot change.

3. Highest are those who are born wise. Next are those who become wise by learning. After them come those who have to work very hard to acquire learning. Finally, to the lowest class of the common people belong those who work very hard without ever managing to learn.

4. The way of the gentleman has three parts: Being human he has no anxieties; being wise he has no doubts; being brave he has no fear.

5. First and foremost, be faithful to your superiors...

6. To have faults and to be making no effort to change them is to have faults indeed!

7. Never do to others what you would not like them to do to you.

8. (Definition of a good man) In private life, courteous; in public life, diligent; in relationships, loyal.

9. Silence is a friend who will never betray.

10. In education there are no class distinctions.

From *The Analects of Confucius*, translated by Arthur Waley (Vintage Books, 1938)

Name ______________________________

Selections from: *The Tao Te Ching*

8

The supreme good is like water,
which nourishes all things without trying to.
It is content with the low places that people disdain.
Thus it is like the Tao.

In dwelling, live close to the ground.
In thinking, keep to the simple.
In conflict, be fair and generous.
In governing, don't try to control.
In work, do what you enjoy.
In family life, be completely present.

When you are content to be simply yourself
and don't compare or compete,
everybody will respect you.

44

Fame or integrity: which is more important?
Money or happiness: which is more valuable?
Success or failure: which is more destructive?

If you look to others for fulfillment,
you will never be truly fulfilled.
If your happiness depends on money,
you will never be happy with yourself.

Be content with what you have;
rejoice in the way things are.
When you realize there is nothing lacking
the whole world belongs to you.

CHAPTER 3

THE HISTORY OF CHINA

Goals for the Unit

Concepts

1. Past events affect how we live and think today.
2. Change is inevitable and has both positive and negative consequences.
3. Present-day attitudes and perspectives influence how we interpret and understand history.
4. Historical events have multiple causes and effects.

Skills

1. Use chronologies, timelines, and historical maps to understand and to record events over time.
2. Read and understand historical text and primary source material.
3. Use historical accounts and primary source material to understand multiple perspectives and for analysis, discussion, and debate.
4. Use artifacts, visual material, and music to deepen and broaden historical understanding.

Background Information

The History of China

Chinese history goes back over 4,000 years. It would be overwhelming to undertake a historical study of such magnitude. To get an overall picture of what occurred in China throughout this extensive period of time, students need to be familiar with the dynamics of traditional Chinese society and the patterns which shaped it.

In order to understand what happened in China during its thousands of years of history, we need to learn how Chinese society was ordered, what its values and priorities were, and how the Chinese viewed their world.

The Social Classes in Traditional Society

According to Confucian theory, there were four major social classes, arranged in importance according to their usefulness to the society at large. Keep in mind that Chinese society was unlike modern societies. Although it had industry as well as commerce, it was not an industrialized society.

Of the four main social classes, the highest was that of the scholars and officials. These people were called Mandarins by Westerners; the term comes from the Portuguese word for "command." Scholar-officials were selected through government-conducted examinations (civil service examinations) which were started at about 200 B.C. There were three successive levels of exams—district, provincial, and national—but all of them were based on the same body of material, early Confucian texts. No women were allowed to take the exams.

Passing the exams allowed one to serve in government, the main avenue to wealth and power, prestige, and status. In theory, anyone could take these exams and, if he passed, enter government service. While some men did manage to climb the social ladder, the successful candidates usually were from families who were officeholders and had the desire and the money to provide for the education of their sons. This class never comprised more than 10 percent of the population.

The second highest class consisted of farmers and peasants, a group that made up more than 70 percent of the population. Peasants provided the economic base of the country, and were therefore respected, at least in principle. In fact, the peasants were subject to exploitation, as well as natural and man-made disasters. Normally, taxes and rent alone took about 50 percent of the value of their crops.

Farmers practiced intensive family agriculture. Small plots were cultivated by family workers, who mostly raised grains such as rice, wheat, millet, and barley. (Slaves were never economically important in China, although they did exist, mainly as house servants.) Because of the increasing population and the practice of dividing land evenly among sons, land was always highly valued, even as the amount of it in cultivation constantly expanded. This gave rise to tenant farmers, who usually rented from scholar-officials who, in turn, had invested in land. Thus there was a direct connection between scholar-officials and landowners, often called "gentry."

The third class was the artisans, people who made things with their hands. They were respected and were concentrated for the most part in cities; they worked within organizations like guilds.

The lowest class was the merchants. Often itinerant, they were scorned as "parasites," who worked with neither their heads nor their hands. It was believed that they encouraged people to buy things they didn't need.

Cities were political centers, not economic ones. Although some merchants became extremely wealthy, surplus wealth, whether of merchants or scholar-officials, was invested in land, not in commercial activity. In fact, successful merchants usually strove to get their sons into the scholar-gentry class.

There was no free, private economy. The government restricted trade and controlled the major production of essential products, such as salt, through government monopolies.

An ongoing problem was the growing concentration of land in the hands of the scholar-gentry. Land was taken off the tax rolls by gentry officials, and government attempts to limit land holdings per family always failed due to a conflict of interests.

Soldiers, Women, Priests, and Emperors

The Chinese attitude toward the military was that of Confucius: The military should not exist in a well-run society, so there was no official class position for the military. Decent people avoided the military. Most soldiers were conscripted peasants.

Women were considered inferior to men. They could not inherit property. The best way for a woman in traditional society to raise her status was to have sons, the more the better. Only sons could perform sacrifices for the ancestors, and only sons carried on the family name.

There was also no organized priesthood in ancient China. Members of the family performed rituals of respect to their ancestors. Nor was there a general religion common to all groups. Although Daoism and Buddhism had priests, reflecting the influence of Buddhism, Confucianism, with its attitude of "respect the spirits but keep your distance," was dominant for most of Chinese history.

The emperor was the highest authority in the land. All officials-scholar-gentry were subordinate to and owed him loyalty. He was called the "Son of Heaven," all-powerful in theory, but in fact, his control of government depended on his personality. The emperor was a member of a hereditary ruling family known as a dynasty. The names of a dynasty was not the family surname, but rather a name chosen to symbolize something good. Names of dynasties are used to describe periods of Chinese history.

Patterns in Chinese History

There are three major factors in Chinese history. The first is the "dynastic cycle." This is a term used to describe the establishment, consolidation, expansion, flowering, fading, decline, and fall of a ruling family. This was considered an inevitable pattern for every dynasty, whether it spanned many centuries or only a few years.

The "Mandate of Heaven" was the term used to rationalize the dynastic cycle. The founder of a dynasty had the "mandate," or command, of heaven to rule. The reason he succeeded in establishing a new dynasty was because heaven willed it to be so, as he was a worthy ruler. The fall of a dynasty, on the other hand, indicated that this ruling family had lost the mandate. Heaven then waited for a more worthy successor. Periods between the effective end of one dynasty and the establishment of a new one were often full of chaos.

The second factor was the movement of the population from north to south. The Yellow River was the cradle of Chinese civilization. By 500 B.C., China already encompassed the Yangtze River valley. The Chinese moved south to avoid wars and invasions, and to find rich agricultural land.

The ongoing uneasy relationships between Chinese and non-Chinese nomadic people of the North and Northwest was the third factor. The Chinese were an agricultural people, engaged primarily in grain production. Due to the drier climate, this culture could not spread to the North and Northwest as it could and did spread to the south. The people of the north and Northwest practiced a pastoral life, raising cattle, sheep, and horses. Their way of life was sharply different from that of the Chinese. The Chinese looked down on them as "barbarians," claiming they did not properly respect age or parents.

There was actually competition, both economic and political, between these two peoples. The Great Wall, which stretched from 1,500 to 1,800 miles, was an unsuccessful attempt to separate the nomads from the Chinese. Each group tried to impose its way of life on the other. Success for one or the other tended to depend on the dynastic cycle in China, a pattern broken only by the coming of the West.

Talking About:
Organizing Group Work

Working with groups is among the most difficult things we ask students to do. Issues that arise include our expectations of students with differing skills and abilities, the management of tasks, conflict resolution, and assessment. Here are some of our own guidelines and strategies:

Choosing Groups

We don't think any one grouping strategy will work all the time. We do think that a group should work together on more than one project. Our students are seated at tables (We call them core groups.). We call upon students in core groups to work together on a variety of activities often, so members get to know one another as workers and we get to know them. We switch core groups only two or three times over the course of the year because of this.

At the beginning of the year, we collect ballots from students on which each student requests four or five tablemates. We try to arrange the groups so that each student has at least one of those. We tell students before they choose that if a friendship turns out to be a distraction rather than an asset, we will rearrange the grouping.

After a few months, when we have observed how students work, we make a second grouping, seating children in configurations we think will work. Comfort in a new class of children who don't know each other well guides grouping at first, so there may be tables of all girls or all boys. By mid-year, however, we arrange the groups so there is diversity in each group. At the same time, we look for combinations of students we think will complement each other.

Roles in Groups

For groups to work, the teacher has to be a part-time sociologist. She has to watch each group work, so she can make informal observations of the various members. We have taken children aside who have helpful social skills and complimented them, or given them tips on how to be more effective. Likewise, we have sometimes given private suggestions for words quieter children can use to enter the discussion or get their own needs met in a group where others are more assertive. We've also encouraged groups to find productive ways to confront groupmates who aren't doing their share of the work.

Dividing Work

If the group works together over a period of time, it's more likely that the strengths of all the members will emerge. If the group is going to work on just one project, it's helpful if you can build in a range of challenges so that there is a greater likelihood that everyone will be able to contribute something.

One reason students work in groups is to learn how to do so. But it is demoralizing to be in a group when you have little to contribute. If Renee, an artistically gifted student, takes on leadership when the group is working on an art piece, and another student helps her with the writing piece, both children are being valued for their contributions.

But if Renee volunteers to make the map, because art is her strength, and Ben writes up the history, because that's his strength, how does Ben improve his art and Renee improve her writing?

If it's impossible or impractical to create an assignment where each of the members has to work in a variety of modes, it's not a terrible thing for members to volunteer to do parts they do well. That imitates life outside of school. Even on school sports teams, specialized tasks are most often assigned to the people who are best at them.

Rules and Expectations

Another common problem is about workload: What happens when the amount of work each person takes on isn't even? What happens if some students aren't working as hard as others? This happens in almost every group, and it is infuriating to the people who work the hardest. Their work ethic and pride comes into conflict with their need not to seem bossy or nagging, or else arguments break out.

We've tried to address this by making the group process itself a manifest goal and objective for which our students are held accountable. At the beginning of a big project, groups meet to divide the work. Sometimes we use a pie chart and ask members to fill it out, privately and together, with their estimates of how much each person will be responsible for. Some children don't mind taking on bigger slices if it is acknowledged in this way. For others, it's a real learning experience for them to see how big or small their part is perceived to be by the rest of the group. Negotiations can take place so that members feel everyone is doing his or her fair share. In follow-up meetings, students can review each others' progress and make comments and adjustments. We are constantly amazed by the power of the collective wisdom that emerges during this process.

Some students, particularly competent ones with good study skills, express anxiety that their grade or assessment will be dependent partly on the work of others, which they judge to be inferior to their own. We try to encourage those students to think as they would on any sports team: people need to learn to cooperate and work together for the good of everyone. However, we usually assess both the team and its members, so that individual efforts may be recognized.

The adjustment to working in groups isn't always easy or fast. Groups that work have members who trust one another, who are aware of each others' strengths, and who communicate well. While this takes time, patience and a sense of humor, what may be learned and accomplished academically and socially is invaluable.

ACTIVITY #1
Dynasty Group Research

Overview
In the course of this project, in which groups of students research different dynasties and create timelines to present their findings, we use a combination of classes including social studies (for planning, discussion, learning and practicing research skills, group meetings), research periods (in the library and using class materials and on-line research), workshop periods (for time on-task), and homework (research, artwork, writing). Students don't work on their research every day; the research project is the main focus, but we learn about other aspects of China while it is progressing.

Goals
1. Students develop knowledge of major historical events in China by constructing a time line.
2. Students learn about the dynastic cycle and to apply that understanding to explain historical continuity and change in China.
3. Students practice group research.

Materials
brown or white mural paper (roll paper or brown "craft paper"), yardsticks, thick black felt-tip pens, colored pencils, markers and paints, Chronology of Dynasties (page 50), Research Organizer reproducible (page 51), map of China (page 22)

Procedure
1. Before getting started, you may want to read "Organizing Group Work" (page 42) and "Research with Middle School Children" (page 30).

2. Hand out copies of Chronology of Chinese Dynasties and discuss the chart with the class. Ask students to speculate why some dates are prefaced by B.C. and A.D., and discuss the meaning of these.

3. Divide the class into nine groups, one for each of the major dynasties (Shang, Zhou, Qin, Han, Tang, Song, Yuan, Ming, and Qing). With an exceptionally large class, you might add

Sui or even the Period of Disunity. Group size will depend on class size. There should be at least two students but not more than four working on any one dynasty.

4. Explain to students that each group will research and create a timeline for its dynasty. The timeline will feature important people, events, inventions, literature, and art from that time period. Student can use the Research Organizer (page 51) to guide their research. At the end of the project, all of the groups will put their time lines together to create a visual history of China.

5. Each group's first task is to figure out how long a sheet of mural paper they will need to create a timeline for its dynasty. Groups can use a scale of 1 foot (or 30 centimeters) equals 100 years.

6. Students rule out the timeline across the center of the mural paper, which will give them space above and below the line for pictures and text. Students should add 100-year markers.

7. Once students have completed their research, they can add the dates of the dynasty, main events, important people, inventions or scientific discoveries, art, and literature to their timeline. They can illustrate their timelines with portraits, depictions of events, drawings of inventions, and samples of art.

8. Students should use the map of China (page 22) to create a map that shows the historical borders of their dynasty. Students can use different colors to show the extent of land controlled by each successive dynasty. Some dynasties actually extended beyond the areas found on the map, so an outline map of all of Asia may be required.

9. Have students present their work to the class in chronological order. Once a dynasty group has made a presentation, its timeline is added to the growing length of visual Chinese history.

10. Display the maps in one area under the heading "Changing China." You may want to study the variations in the extent of territory controlled by China over the centuries as the subject of a specific lesson.

Follow-up Activities

Inventions Research: Information on science and technology/inventions is incorporated into dynasty research. However, for those who wish to emphasize technology, China is an amazing source of technological innovation. The majority of texts on China mention the most famous: the magnetic compass, paper, printing, and gunpowder. Some sources add tea, silk, or porcelain. A list of some of the less well-known inventions, taken from the Asia Society Web site is below. For more detailed explanations, see this Web site. There are also suggested lesson plans for this topic. The developers of the Web site give credit to Robert Temple's book.

- the horse collar
- the moldboard plow
- cast iron
- the decimal system
- matches
- paper
- the kite
- the wheelbarrow
- paper money
- the helicopter rotor and the propeller
- the seismograph
- circulation of the blood
- brandy and whiskey
- the rocket and multistage rockets

A study of the movement of technology is a complete project in itself. Trade routes such as the famed silk route, the travels of Marco Polo, Arab traders, the Arab conquest of Spain and Portugal, even the Crusades played roles in this saga. Students can research when a particular invention reached the West, and its route of transmission.

Inventions Debate or Essay: Students take simple inventions like the compass or movable type for granted. Also, they may make assumptions about the effect of an invention on a culture. For example, that the culture that invented gunpowder will have a military advantage over neighboring cultures without gunpowder. Information about inventions could be collected together so that all students can access it. Then, have a class discussion about which invention is most important—and exactly what makes an invention important. Some of our students decided gunpowder was important because it enabled a country to conquer another country. Other students said that because it was used to kill people, it didn't deserve to be called important. An essay assignment could follow the discussion or be used in its place.

Museum of Chinese Inventions: Individuals or groups might make diagrams or models of inventions they've researched. Using computer animation, students can show how they work. Books of science experiments have instructions for making working compasses; the block printing described in the name chop project might be extended to illustrate movable type, etc. Students who have visited museums of science and industry or natural history museums could guide their classmates in setting up exhibits of their work.

The Great Wall, Again and Again: This activity can be done with almost any historical event. The idea is to research a topic using a variety of resources. Have students record concrete information on a grid. Who constructed it? When? For what purpose? Of what materials? What were the dimensions? Students usually find that most of the information they find agrees, but some doesn't. Then have a discussion about why there might be disagreement and why it's important to research using many sources.

Teaching Strategies

1. Keeping Track of "Stuff": Since we don't do the Dynasty project in a linear way, a lot of materials are continuously being taken out and put away. We use plastic milk crates, one per group, as containers for each group's resources. Students keep art materials, books, folders of articles, and their notes in the crates, which are labeled with the name of the dynasties. We also have our arts-and-crafts supplies (rulers, scissors, sets of colored pencils) organized into sets; the number of sets is determined by the number of groups. On a rotating basis, group members are required to put away materials and to clean up the area. Timelines are either fastened to the wall in the school hallway, even as works-in-progress, or rolled up and secured with an elastic band.

2. Building a Web Resource Guide: Students doing dynasty research on the Internet often discover Web sites about China we didn't know about. We ask that they bookmark them. Periodically, we open the Bookmarks option in the pull-down menu and drag all the new addresses to the China folder so they are accessible to everyone. These may then be further organized, annotated, renamed and saved as an HTML file.

Activity #2
Integrating Historical Fiction

Overview
Doing a literature study using a related historical novel is a good way to get more curricular bang for your buck: children can practice reading and learn literature-appreciation skills while they develop a richer sense of lifestyle and history. In addition, stories tend to be more engaging than nonfiction text for many students, since they give them an opportunity to think, talk, and write about issues that relate to their own lives.

Goals
1. Students develop literature appreciation skills, build reading comprehension, and practice writing skills.
2. Students practice summary skills.
3. Students make observations about lifestyle and learn more about historical events.

Materials
• a class set of novels

After many years of experience and experimentation, we have returned to *The Good Earth* by Pearl S. Buck. This novel provides a realistic and detailed description of the life of a traditional Chinese peasant within a dramatic and interesting plot. Discussion of this work can focus on aspects of Chinese life as depicted in the story, plot, and characterization.

Procedure
1. We begin by reading the first few pages aloud together, and having a discussion about what we learn, the author's style, and potential difficulties. We talk about what we are told (e.g., it is Wang Lung's wedding day) as opposed to what we may infer (Wang Lung is both excited and anxious). This is a new skill for some readers, and it is one we revisit often.

2. For the first third of the book, we assign review questions: The answers to the literal questions form an approximate summary of the chapter assigned. Inferring questions may refer to historical events, techniques of narration, or making connections or predictions. We also assign journal entries with topics that relate events in the story to students' own lives.

3. In the second third of the book, we ask students to make chapter summaries two or three times a week. Each student writes four summaries of each chapter as follows: 1.) 100 to 150 words long; 2.) 50 to 75 words long; 3.) a one-sentence summary; 4.) a new title. We talk first about the qualities of a good summary and strategies students may use. Students read their summaries aloud and we review them for accuracy and technique.

4. We don't usually make written assignments for the last third of the book. There is considerable plot momentum by then; students want to know what's going to happen and they become tired of completing a writing activity each time they read.

5. Once the reading is completed, we spend one period debriefing with a round-robin discussion in which every student is encouraged to respond to the book in one or two sentences. We record the responses on chart paper.

6. Next, we divide into groups; each is responsible for several chapters. Going back over the book, the groups find information about culture, lifestyle, and historical events. This information is collected on notes and reproduced for the class, or written on chart paper, which is posted for the class to review.

7. The style of the writing usually suggests our literature appreciation skills goals. If, for example, an author is strong at characterization through dialogue we might focus on that. We review the basic elements of fiction and then examine how the author used events and culture in the plot and setting of the novel. Between the curricular framework in language arts for your school, the abilities of your students, and the style of the author, your literature appreciation goals will probably emerge.

Teaching Strategies

1. Responding to Literature: What are your goals in asking students to write the answers to questions about a reading? Among those we've incorporated into assignments are the following: practice at using the question to frame an answer; writing good sentences; recalling information; summarizing; locating information; relating the reading to the students' lives; grammar; proofreading; and handwriting.

2. Integrating the Book Into Your Unit: To an extent, we allow the cultural issues that arise in the course of the reading to determine when we study them. For example, in *The Good Earth*, Olan decides that her second daughter will have her feet bound. At this point in the story, we read other material about foot binding and discuss the implications of this practice in light of what students know about the role of women in traditional China.

3. Handling Challenging Reading Assignments: *The Good Earth* is difficult reading for some students. One way we've dealt with this is by purchasing the audiotape version of the book and lending it out or providing time in school for students to listen as they read. With books that aren't available on audio, we've made our own audiotapes, employing students, parents, and student teachers as readers. We dub these to have multiple copies as needed.

Follow-up Activities

Responding to Literature: We often mix art, drama and writing activities in the course of the reading and as well as afterward. Some projects we might assign are:
- illustrate a scene
- draw a portrait of a character from a description
- have a panel of reporters interview a character
- improvise a scene from the book; discuss how students have portrayed characters

- make a movie poster including a scene from the book and suitable actors to play the roles
- have a debate or a trial involving an issue or character

Extension Activities

Literature: Try a Chinese Mystery

Robert Van Gulik (1910–1967), a Dutch authority on Chinese history and culture, wrote about 20 detective novels based on the legendary exploits of Ti Jen-chieh, Judge Dee, a real Tang Dynasty magistrate who became the subject of detective novels in China in the 17th century. In the Tang Dynasty, the magistrate served as the head of the police force, the detective, the judge, and the jury. If he erred, he had to suffer the punishment that would otherwise have been meted out to the guilty party. In personality and method, Judge Dee is not unlike Sherlock Holmes or Hercule Poirot. The novels are fun, and since they are set in ancient China, there is much to be learned about the lifestyle and the legal system of the day. In conjunction with this, we read, *Two-Minute Mysteries*, by Donald Sobel and others, and talk about the craft of mystery writing. At the end of the unit, students write short Judge Dee mysteries of their own.

Name ____________________

Chronology of Chinese Dynasties

Dates	**Dynasty**
ca. 21st-16th century B.C.	Xia (Hsia); sometimes called Yin
ca. 1600-1027 B.C.	Shang
1027-221 B.C. 1027-771 B.C. 770-221 B.C. 770-476 B.C. 476-221 B.C.	Zhou (Chou) Western Zhou Eastern Zhou Spring and Autumn Period Warring States Period
221-206 B.C.	Qin
202 B.C.-A.D. 220 202 B.C.-A.D. 9 9-24 25-220	Han Western Han Wang Mang Interregnum Eastern Han
220-581 220-280 220-265 265-581	Period of Disunity Three Kingdoms Wei Jin (Chin)
581-618	Sui
618-907	Tang
907-960	Five Dynasties
960-1279 960-1127 947-1125 1127-1279 1125-1234	Song (Sung) Northern Song Liao Southern Song Jin (Chin)
1279-1368	Yuan = Mongols
1368-1644	Ming
1644-1911	Qing (Ch'ing) = Manchus

The dates given for the early dynasties vary. From the Qin Dynasty on, they are the same on most dynasty charts.

Name ______________________________

Organizing Your Research

Group Members:	Tasks Timeline: • Important people • Important events • Inventions • Map	Due Dates:
Name of Dynasty:	Dates:	
(Names of) Important People?	Birth/Death Dates?	Why Important?
Major Events: What happened?	When?	Why Important?
Inventions: What and When?		
Literature: Most famous title(s)?	Author(s)?	What was it?
Art and/or architecture: Most famous?	Picture:	

CHAPTER 4

LANGUAGE AND WRITING

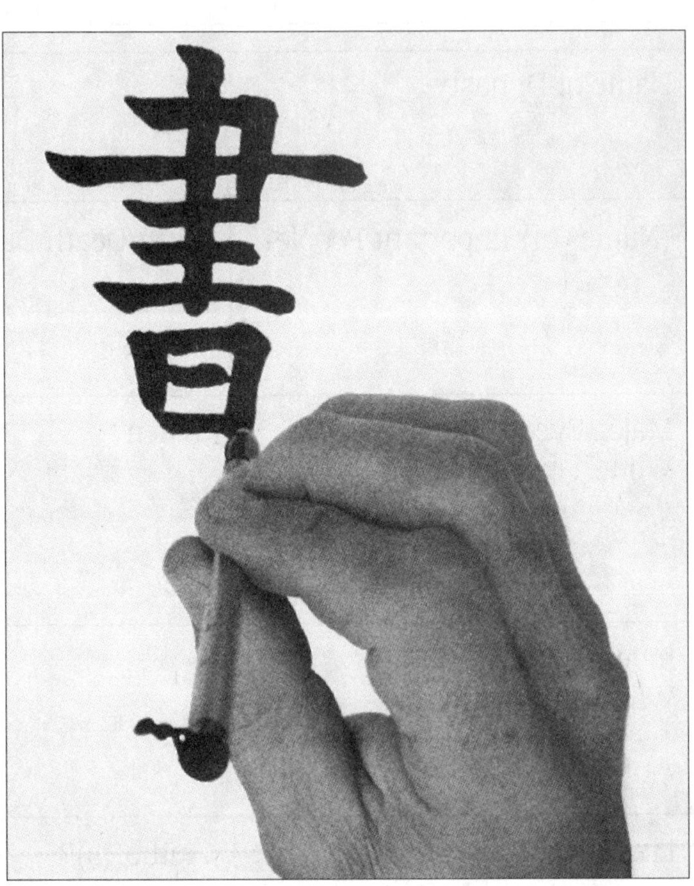

Goals for the Unit

Concepts

1. Language is a system of communication.
2. All languages have rules for correct speech.
3. Writing takes forms other than the alphabet we use in the West.
4. Geographic barriers cause variations in speech (dialects) within a country.

Skills

1. Compare characteristics of the Chinese language with our own.
2. Experiment with different writing materials.
3. Read and write some Chinese characters.

Background Information

Language and Writing

Mandarin and Chinese Dialects

Communication in premodern China was difficult not only because the country was so large, but because its many crisscrossing mountain ranges and great rivers further hampered access between communities. Consequently, areas of China that were cut off from one another developed variations in language (dialects). The major ones are Mandarin, Cantonese, Fujianese (Fukienese), the Wu dialect of the Shanghai area, and Hakka. In many ways, these dialects are as different from one another as French is from Italian. Standard Chinese, also called

Mandarin, which is based on a northern dialect, is most widespread. It is spoken in some form or other throughout north China, and in some areas of central China. In modern times, successive Chinese governments have all sought to establish and enforce a single standard Chinese pronunciation.

Standard Chinese is the official language of China, and is based on the Chinese spoken in the area around Beijing, the capital. In English, this form of Chinese is called Mandarin, because it was the language of the official class in traditional times. Obviously, it was necessary for officials to be able to communicate with one another, no matter where in China they were from, or where in China they served.

Characteristics of the Chinese Language

Many people in the West view Chinese as a mysterious, inscrutable language, impossible to decipher unless you are Chinese. The fact that there is no alphabet seems chaotic or primitive. However, as in every other language, there are rules as well as specific characteristics that hold true whatever the dialect.

Spoken Chinese

Chinese is a tonal language. The pitch of the voice when saying a word imparts some of its meaning. Changing the tone of a word always changes its meaning. In Mandarin there are four different tones (level, rising, dipping, falling), but in other Chinese dialects there can be as many as eight. Cantonese, until recent times the most frequently heard form of Chinese in the United States, has seven tones. This is the reason Chinese sounds "sing-song" to English speakers. Tonal Western languages, such as Swedish, also sound that way to us.

Other characteristics of Chinese may help explain certain mistakes often made by native Chinese when they write or speak English. One is that the Chinese language doesn't change the form of nouns to indicate plurals, nor do verbs change form because of tense or person. A few examples are: "ta" means "he," "she," or "it." "Ma" is "horse" or "horses." "Zou" is "go," "will go," or "went." Context words are used to specify meaning. However, Chinese word order is very similar to English.

Chinese write their names with the family name first, then the personal name. This reflects the Chinese view that the family is more important than the individual.

Written Chinese

The Chinese written language does not use an alphabet. It is written using characters, which represent ideas or sometimes syllables. Originally pictographs or pictures, they were simplified, added to, or made more abstract, and so evolved into the forms used today.

The written language is the same no matter what dialect the speaker uses or, for that matter, whether it is an entirely different language, like Japanese. This is like the numbers 1, 2, 3.

You may pronounce them in different ways, depending on what language you speak, but the meaning is the same. Written language is not only a unifying factor in Chinese culture, but also a historical unifier, as an unbroken tradition of writing goes back about 4,000 years.

The earliest writings in China are found inscribed on "oracle bones" (questions written on shoulder bones or tortoiseshells which were then used for divination), as inscriptions cast in bronze, and written on wood, bamboo and silk. And calligraphy, or "beautiful writing," is the mark of an educated, cultivated person and an art form as well.

PEACE

The value placed on writing is shown by the "Four Treasures" of a scholar's study: the ink and inkstone, brush pen, and paper—the basic tools of Chinese writing. Nowadays one can buy liquid ink as well as ink sticks, but traditionally ink came in solid sticks, often decorated with designs or characters which made them art objects in themselves. The ink stick was ground on an inkstone with a little water. An inkstone is a flat stone with a hollow scooped out where the liquid ink collects. As with the ink stick, inkstones were made as artistically as possible. A brush pen is made of animal hair, tied together in small bunches and fixed into a hollow handle. Brushes use the hair of different animals—sheep and rabbit are common—depending on the way the calligrapher wants the characters to look. Paper, a Chinese invention, is the last of the treasures. Many special and beautiful kinds of paper are used for calligraphy and painting.

Characters traditionally were written from the top of the page to the bottom, starting in the upper-right-hand corner. Books opened with the binding on the right. Now most books published in China print characters horizontally, usually from left to right. The number of characters is more than 70,000, but most people only need to master 3,000 to 4,000 characters in order to read fluently.

Traditionally, no punctuation as we know it in the West was used, no space was left between words or sentences, and there were no indications, like capitals, of which words were proper nouns. Classical Chinese used special words or balanced phrases to tell the reader how to "punctuate." Although Chinese today uses a type of Western-style punctuation, there are still no spaces between words, and no special way of telling which word is a proper noun.

It is often said that Chinese is monosyllabic, but this is true only of the traditional written language, called literary or classical Chinese, in which the meaning is perfectly clear from one character because of its visual nature. Spoken Chinese uses multisyllable words, and since the early part of this century writers have reflected the spoken form of the language in their work.

The language continues to change with the times. In the People's Republic of China, in order to increase literacy, a conscious effort has been made to simplify characters by reducing the number of strokes needed to write them, or by standardizing the phonetic parts. Often these changes are based on earlier cursive forms, but sometimes entirely new versions of characters are created.

In addition, today's Chinese language borrows words from other languages in several ways. Either the meaning is translated, as in "electric brain" meaning "computer," or characters are found to represent the sound, as in "dun" meaning "ton."

Written Chinese influenced other cultures in East Asia. Japan and Korea both borrowed and used Chinese characters to write languages that were completely different from Chinese. Both countries eventually developed scripts more suited to their own languages, but even today "kanji" or "Han words" remain an important component of written Japanese.

Activity #1

Calligraphy Workshop

Overview

Students practice writing Chinese characters using calligraphy pens.

Goals

1. Students reinforce information learned about written Chinese.
2. Students experience using the traditional tools of Chinese writing.

Materials

- charts of Chinese characters (You can use any of the characters on pages 63-65 for this activity)
- blank white paper
- medium-sized calligraphy brush pens, one for each student (You can buy these from any art supplier. Don't buy ones already inked.)
- one inkstone and one ink stick
- 1 quart of black ink
- small paper cups for ink and water
- paper towels at each table to absorb excess water or ink on pens, or to mop up spills

Procedure

1. Demonstrate how to grind ink using a traditional ink stick and inkstone and let each student have a chance to do it.
Method: Put a little tap water on the inkstone. Dip one end of the ink stick in the water, move to the raised area of the stone, and rub gently. Repeat the process until the water is dark enough for writing.

2. Cover desks or tabletops with newspaper and secure with masking tape. Have children bring in old shirts to use as smocks. We've rarely had spills, but the ink we use is permanent. Paper plates or sticks made of taped, rolled-up newspaper make good brush rests. Explain to your students that if they stand the long brushes in the short cups of ink, their cups may tilt and spill.

3. Put a small amount of liquid ink into each of the small paper cups, one for each group of two or three students. Put a small amount of water in another cup.

4. We use 8 $^1/_2$–by–11–inch white paper folded into 8 or 16 boxes. You don't have to use expensive rice paper, but construction paper is too absorbent. Ask students to put their names on five or six sheets of paper in pencil before beginning to write with ink so that they may be reunited with their work later.

5. To write, students should dip their brush pens in the water cup first, wiping them off on the edge of the cup, then dip them in the ink cup, then wipe again before beginning to use them for writing.

6. Explain to students the position of the brush in the hand: The shaft of the brush remains perpendicular to the paper, held with the four fingers and with the thumb extended. There is more movement of wrist and arm and less of the small muscles of the fingers as in Western writing. It is important to sit up straight with both feet on the floor when writing with a brush pen. Once the stroke is begun, it is followed to its conclusion and left alone—no sketchy lines or filling in later. The strokes should be slightly broader at the end than in the middle. This is accomplished by varying the pressure on the brush.

7. Hand out copies of Common Chinese Name and Characters reproducible for students to copy.

8. Place students' work on a countertop or windowsill to dry.

9. Begin cleanup ten minutes before the end of the session. Have one person from each table take the leftover ink and pour it carefully into a pitcher you've put out. Have another student collect the brushes and put them into a bucket of warm soapy water. Have the remaining students transfer finished papers to the drying place and remove the newspaper lining from the desktops.

Teaching Strategies

1. Emphasizing Practice and Concentration: We emphasize that calligraphers practice the strokes and characters many thousands of times before they are taken seriously as artists. We insist on quiet for concentration, and have the students repeat the same characters at least 16 times before trying new ones. We ask them to circle the ones they feel came out best.

2. Modeling Chinese Characters: You can model the order of the strokes by "painting" with water on the chalkboard with a larger brush such as those most common to early childhood classrooms.

Follow-up Activities

Simple Sentences: Challenge students to write simple sentences using as many of the characters as they can.

Living Characters: Reinforce the shapes of Chinese characters by having students use their bodies to make their shapes. Three students are best—one shorter and 2 taller students. Have students sit or stand, sometimes in front of each other, to create the characters.

Activity #2
A Chinese Folktale Rebus

Overview
Students reading a Chinese folktale.

Goals
1. Students practice reading some common Chinese characters.
2. Students read a Chinese trickster tale.
3. Students use drama or creative writing to solve a problem.

Materials
• "Soo Tan the Tiger and the Little Green Frog" reproducibles (pages 61-63)

Procedure
1. Pass out copies of the Chinese characters reprodicble (page 63). Have students look at the characters.

2. Hand out copies of "Soo Tan the Tiger and the Little Green Frog" to students. Read the first sentence or two of the story with your students. Direct them to the characters sheet and explain that they may look at it to remind them of the meaning of the characters in the story.

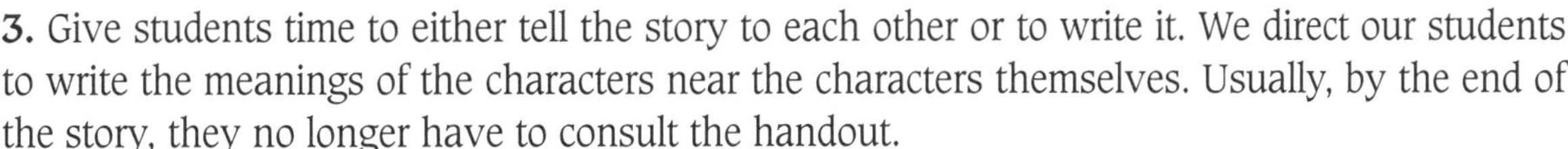

3. Give students time to either tell the story to each other or to write it. We direct our students to write the meanings of the characters near the characters themselves. Usually, by the end of the story, they no longer have to consult the handout.

4. Read the story together. Elicit from the students the observation that the frog is inferior in strength to the tiger and so he uses his cleverness and trickery to outwit his enemy. Introduce the term "trickster tale" if your students are unfamiliar with it.

5. Ask students if they can name any other tricksters, such as Bre'r Rabbit, from folk literature or in the popular media.

Follow-up Activities
Writing, Part Two: Explain to the class that in the second part of the story, the tiger meets a fox who challenges him to return and kill the frog. Have groups of three students (the tiger, the fox, and the frog) discuss a possible ending to the story, and then act it out for the rest of the class. Another alternative is to have individuals write an ending to the story.

Activity #3
Making a Name Chop

Overview
Students chose a Chinese name and create a Name Chop (a stamp with their name.) of their new name.

Goals
1. Students reinforce information learned about written Chinese
2. Students learn or reinforce information learned about naming in China

Materials
- Common Chinese Names chart (page 64)
- tracing paper
- flat sheets of Styrofoam (cut 1 $^1/_2$ inch squares from thoroughly cleaned supermarket meat trays.)
- art knives or sharp pencils (for use with Styrofoam)
- red acrylic paint, or a red ink pad
- flat plastic trays, or some other stiff, nonabsorbent boards
- small brayers (handheld inking rollers)

Procedure
1. Students begin by selecting Chinese names for themselves using the Common Chinese Names chart. A single character for the family name is standard. Remind students that it always comes before the pesonal name. Personal names may be selected according to preference. In general, flowers or gemstones are used for girls' names. Characters for qualities like boldness and courage tend to be used for boys. The character "yang" is definitely associated with boys, the character "yin" with girls. While most Chinese names use two characters for personal names, one-character names are also very common. Today in China, when names are written in romanization, the last name comes first, then two personal names written together as one word, for example, Deng Xiaoping. The seals are easier to make if the characters are not too complicated.

2. Once students have selected their names, they should trace its characters onto the tracing paper. Depending on the shape of the "seal," put the family name on top, and the two personal names lined up under it; or put the family name on the right side and the two characters for the personal name one above the other on the left side. Reverse the tracing paper and put it on the Styrofoam. Puncture the tracing paper along the lines of each character to produce a reverse image of the characters on the seal. An art knife will make very clear lines but students can also use pencils to mark the lines. Mark which side is "up"on the back of the seal.

3. Put red acrylic paint on plastic trays and roll it out to spread it evenly. Students press their seals onto the trays, or run the inked brayer over the seal. The seal can then be stamped.

Practice pressing the seal on scrap paper to test it. If it is not clear, etch the lines more clearly. Alternatively, use the red ink pad. The latter is easier to use and makes a finer print, but the color isn't as bright.

Teaching Strategy

Working with Art Materials: How often do your students work with art materials? Is this a comfortable activity for you? If, for example, you are anxious about using razor-sharp tools, how can you become more at ease? Should you use the Styrofoam and pencil method instead? Or can you spend some time talking about how to, and how not to, use an art knife? Make sure students understand that clowning around can be dangerous and won't be tolerated.

Follow-up Activities

Using the Name Chop: Allow students to stamp other schoolwork with their chop. (Keep the red ink pad handy. It's quicker and easier than the paint.) Save the chop for signatures when students make scroll paintings and write poetry.

Make a Name Dictionary: Create a dictionary of class Chinese names using index cards, on which students write their Western names, the English translation of their Chinese names, and stamp their chop. Post these.

ACTIVITY #4
"Translating" Poetry

Overview
Because of the structure of Chinese, translating poetry may be a highly interpretive exercise. This activity gives students a sense of both the difficulty and the creativity of the process.

Goals
- To help students understand the difficulty of translating from one language into another.
- To appreciate the skill required to turn exact meaning into poetry.
- To create poetry from existing material.

Materials
- Deer Enclosure (page 65)
- Professional translation of the same poem (see next page)

Procedure
1. Students read the literal meaning of the words in the poem by Wang Wei found on the handout.
2. Using the handout as a worksheet, students attempt to "translate" the literal meaning of the Chinese words into a four-line poem in English. Direct them to try to keep a consistent meaning for the poem, as they understand it.

3. Students should then try to polish the poem so that it reads like poetry. It does not need to rhyme. They might use a thesaurus to find more colorful or precise words.

4. When students are satisfied, they should recopy the poem neatly and illustrate it in color.

5. Students should share their translations and discuss differences in interpretation.

6. Share with students the professional translation below. Students might then compare their poetic renditions with a professional translation. Discuss the differences.

Deer Forest Hermitage by Wang Wei

Through the deep wood, the slanting sunlight
Casts motley patterns on the jade-green mosses.
No glimpse of man in this lonely mountain,
Yet faint voices drift on the air.

Teaching Strategies

Getting Students Comfortable with Sharing: How comfortable are your students with sharing their writing aloud? Often the same few students may volunteer. Sometimes, if their writing even seems to be competent, it may intimidate and silence others. Here are some suggestions:

• Have students post their poems around the classroom. Then allow time for everyone to circulate and read their classmates' work. Encourage note taking. Then discuss the poems.

• Ask students to share in small groups instead of in front of the whole class. Afterward, you might say, "Did anyone hear a poem they'd like to encourage the writer to read aloud?" Sometimes with that extra support, a writer will be willing to take a chance.

• Make rules for what students are allowed to do and say about another's work. Do you want work applauded? Do you allow put-downs or inappropriate laughter? Your class is looking to you as the guardian of safe airways.

• One technique to keep things moving when we have a lot of short pieces is to tell students to listen for one or two things they like about the piece. After the writer reads, he or she calls on two people to share those positive observations. Alternatively, we've distributed scrap paper. Each time a writer reads, listeners jot down one or two positive observations, sign them, and pass them to the writer.

Name ____

Soo Tan the Tiger and the Little Green Frog Part 1

Once when the world was young, animals could talk to each other in their 林 homes.

Soo Tan was an old 虎 who used to wander around the 林 in search of 食. One 日, he came down from the 山, and as he was snuffling along a 河 bank, a 小青蛙 began to croak at him. From his mound of mud and grass, he called, "So, 虎, where might you be going on this beautiful 日?"

But to himself, he said, "虎 has certainly come here to 吃 me! If I am to save myself, I must use my wits."

Soo Tan the 虎 answered, "I am going to the 林 to find some 食. It has been 三 or 四 日 since I have 吃, and I am tired and hungry. As a matter of fact, I think I will 吃 you, even though you are just a morsel for me. But first tell me who you are."

The 小青蛙 blew up his belly and croaked, "I am the 王 of the Frogs. I can 跳 very far and do all sorts of other wonderful things. Look here—there is a 河. Let us have a contest to see who can 跳 farther across it."

As the 虎 was preparing for his 跳, the 小青蛙 snuck around and grabbed hold of the 虎 tail with his mouth. When the 虎 跳, he didn't notice that he had carried the 蛙 across the

Name ____

Soo Tan the Tiger and the Little Green Frog Part 2

河 with him. He turned around to see where the 蛙 was and was surprised to hear the 蛙 croaking behind him. "Looking for something, Soo Tan?" he said.

The 虎 was amazed to see the 小青蛙 so far out in front of him.

"Well, then, Soo Tan," the 蛙 said. "Since I have beaten you in jumping, let us have another contest. This time spitting!"

Soo Tan accepted the challenge, although his huge mouth was dry because he had had nothing to 吃 in days. He tried and tried, but only a 小水 trickled down from the side of his mouth.

Now it was the 小青蛙 turn, and he spit out a big ball of 虎 hair which he had bitten off as they flew across the 河 .

"Why do you have 虎 hair in your stomach?" Soo Tan asked.

"Well," said the 蛙 , yesterday I killed a 虎 and 吃 him, and these hairs here are just the few I could not digest."

Soo Tan thought to himself: "My, the 蛙 must be very strong indeed to kill a 虎 ! And he also can 跳 farther than a 虎 . I must escape while I still have the chance!" And at that, he turned and ran up the path through the 林 to the highest part of the 山 where the 蛙 would not follow and bother him further.

Name ______________________________

Soo Tan the Tiger and the Little Green Frog

day	日	green	青
food	食	frog	蛙
forest, woods	林	tiger	虎
stream	河	eat	吃
little, small	小	three	三
four	四	jump	跳
one	一	mountain	山
king	王	water	水

Name ____________________

Common Chinese Names

						Last Names
大	dà (big)	夫	fū (sage, distinguished person)	長	cháng (long, excelling)	Yáng 羊
天	tiān (heaven)	龍	lúng (dragon)	好	hǎo (good)	Kǒ 可
安	án (peace)	偉	wěi (admirable, extraordinary)	兒	ér (son, child)	Wǔ 伍
月	yuè (moon)	石	shíh (stone)	子	zǐ (child)	Lái 來
花	huà (flower)	黑	hēi (black)	士	shìh (scholar, gentleman)	Fāng 方
玉	yū (jade)	風	fēng (wind)	明	míng (bright, brilliant)	Máo 毛
全	jīn (gold)	達	dá (intelligent, successful)	甫	fǔ (eminent, great)	Jíng 井
銀	yín (silver)	統	tǒng (govern, rule)	日	rì (sun)	Lěng 冷
清	chīng (clear, pure)	英	yíng (brave, heroic)			Rén 任
娘	níang (girl, woman)					Shēn 申

Name ______________________________

"Deer Enclosure"

	鹿 **"Deer**	柴 **Enclosure"**		
空 Empty	山 mountain	不 not	見 see	人， man,
但 but	聞 hear	人 man	語 voice	響。 sound.
返 Reflecting	景 shadow	入 enter	深 deep	林， forest,
復 Again/and	照 shine	青 green	苔 moss	上。 upon.

Literal translation of a Chinese poem of the Tang dynasty

CHAPTER 5

PAINTING AND OTHER ART

Goals for the Unit

Concepts

1. Art reflects the philosophies of the society in which it is created. In China, art reflected the views of Daoists, Buddhists, and Confucians.
2. Painting, especially landscape painting, was considered the highest form of art because of its connection with writing.
3. Chinese art looks different from Western art because of differences in materials and techniques as well as in underlying world views.
4. The Chinese view is that even everyday items can be beautiful as well as useful.

Skills

1. Compare and contrast traditional Chinese painting with Western painting.
2. Appreciate the role of tradition in the techniques and subjects of Chinese painting.

Background Information

Art in Traditional China

China has one of the great artistic traditions of the world, dating from prehistoric times. All artists express their views of the world, whether they be aspects of daily life or as spiritual meaning. Chinese art has generally emphasized symbolism over reality, skill over originality. Chinese artists have sought unity and harmony of people and nature, and their works have strongly reflected the philosophical underpinnings of Chinese society, particularly the Daoist view of the world (see Philosophy and Religion).

In China, the ideal artist was an amateur, not a professional. The scholar/official was a painter and calligrapher. The people who created the magnificent Chinese ceramics, jade, bronze, and metalwork were artisans. Their work was infused with the idea that things should be beautiful as well as useful.

Scroll Painting

For the Chinese, landscape painting was the highest form of art. It used the same materials as writing: the brush pen, ink, and paper made of mulberry bark, rice straw, or silk. The medium, ink on absorbent paper or silk, meant that there was no change possible once a line was drawn. The artist had to see the picture he wanted to create in his own mind before he began. The use of ink rather than paint also encouraged monochrome painting, although colored washes (water-based paints) were freely used in many periods. Line was very important. Artists did not depict shadows because a shadow is a momentary phenomenon; instead, the direction of the light is shown by a slightly thicker line. The connection between writing and painting was also indicated by the addition of calligraphy to most paintings. Beautiful writing was considered an art form in itself, and the addition of a poem or comment in the artist's hand expressed the mood of a painting.

There was no attempt to go out into nature and paint a scene on site, or to use models. The Chinese view of the artistic process emphasized processing the scene through the mind in order to get at its true essence. So the artist painted in his studio or from memory. It was neither necessary nor desirable for the painting to represent a specific place, even though the place which inspired the artist might be recorded in a poem or caption.

The Chinese made no attempt to pretend a painting was anything other than two-dimensional. The reasoning was that paper is flat, so a painting should be flat. Perspective consisted of expansion in the distance. Close elements are at the bottom of the painting; the horizon is toward the top. Distant things are hazy blue or gray.

The artist saw his painting as just a fragment of nature, one that could be cut off at the edge of the paper. The part of nature depicted, however, needed to incorporate certain elements in order to reflect the balance of nature. These were mountains, water, and some indication of people. The people present, however, were always very small in comparison to the natural scene which dominates the painting, thus indicating the insignificance of humans as compared to nature.

An artist was also supposed to eliminate all unnecessary detail. He "suggests" by leaving unpainted areas, and lets the viewer fill in the rest of the scene from his own mind. Generally, these areas are seen as mist, water, or sky. These empty spaces represent the balance in nature between things and nothingness, or the concept of yin and yang. So not all the paper or silk your students are using should be painted on.

Paintings were mounted on scrolls that could be hung or kept rolled up until the viewer wished to look at them. Mountings were paper on the back, beautiful brocaded silk on the front. In keeping with the classic proportion of heaven to earth, a painting had two thirds of the mounting on top, and one third on the bottom.

Ceramics

The most famous ceramic product of China, of course, is porcelain. It has very specific and special qualities: it is white (it can be glazed with color), translucent (it lets light through), waterproof, sonorous (it rings when tapped), hard, and the glaze is united with the clay (the glaze won't come off). Porcelain is made from a very white clay fired in an extremely hot kiln.

Beautiful ceramic products do not have to be porcelain. Since Neolithic times, 7,000 years ago, Chinese have been creating fine painted pottery. Through the centuries, Chinese have used the potter's wheel, and have created designs in the clay with molds or carving. Some of the most famous glazes include: celedon green; cobalt blue; "peach bloom" of copper; iron oxides for browns, reds, and yellows. Ceramics were used by ordinary people for tableware, vases, even pillows, and graced the palaces of emperors and aristocracy.

Another use for ceramics was as tomb figures. In very ancient times, people and animals were sometimes sacrificed and entombed with their masters. Valuable objects were also put into the grave. By the Warring States Period, this practice had given way to burying models of people, animals and property to accompany and serve the dead person in the afterworld. Skillfully crafted houses and pavilions, farms and barnyards, horses and camels depict life 1,000 to 2,000 years ago. We can also see how people dressed, what they did for amusement, and entertainment, and what they did for a living.

Jade

Jade is another substance closely linked to the Chinese. The name is commonly given to two different minerals, jadeite and nephrite. The first is much more valuable. We usually think of jade as green, but it actually comes in many different colors with names such as: apple green, spinach green, camphor, old snow, mutton fat, and red. Jade is extremely hard, second only to diamond, and so it may not be carved. Rather it is abraded by materials harder than itself, including minerals from some rivers. Its hardness, translucence, luster, and ring make it a symbol of integrity and virtue.

Using Museums to Enhance the Curriculum

We usually plan a museum trip immediately after students have learned about Chinese art. Students are usually awed by the technique and artistry of Chinese calligraphy and painting in ways they wouldn't have been without close study first. To make our museum trip as productive as possible, we plan our activities carefully. We have found that with our sixth and seventh graders two hours of museum activities is the maximum time students can work productively. We also create trip sheets to help students to look closely at the work. For example, we might ask students to copy a detail from a painting. Finally, we integrate related activities into our trips, such as having students write a poem about one of the scroll paintings.

ACTIVITY #1

Comparing Chinese and Western Landscapes

Overview

Students learn the principles behind Chinese landscape painting, as well as the materials and techniques used to paint them, through comparison with more familiar western landscape painting.

Materials

- Graphic Organizer: Comparing Chinese and Western Landscapes (page 71)
- Landscape Scroll Painting (See example on page 66. For more examples, see *Art Treasures of the Peking Museum* (Harry Abrams, 1980.)
- Western Landscape Painting. We've used Winslow Homer's "Gulfstream" and Grant Wood's "Paul Revere's Ride" for this activity. See *Winslow Homer* (Harry Abrams, 1990) for a print of "Gulfstream" and *Teaching American History with Art Masterpieces* (Scholastic Professional Books, 1998) for a print of the Grant Wood work.

Procedure

1. From the resources suggested above, select a Chinese and Western landscape to work with. When selecting a western landscape painting, try to choose one from a realistic school of painting such as the Hudson River School. Avoid impressionist paintings that were influenced by Asian art. Display the paintings side by side where students can all see them.

2. Allow students to take a close look at both paintings and take notes before you begin the class.

3. Hand out copies of the graphic organizer Comparing Chinese and Western Landscapes. Ask students to fill in the page as they compare the different paintings.

4. Begin by discussing the differences between the two styles of paintings. Ask students why they think the differences exist. Are there any similarities?

5. Remind students that Chinese painters were supposed to be amateurs, whereas most famous Western painters tried to earn their living from painting. Ask if they they think this would make a difference in their artistic productions.

6. Discuss the connections between Chinese landscape painting and the Daoist philosophy. Students might want to refer to the graphic organizer they completed. Have students use the landscape painting to support their points.

Name Diane Lentine

Comparing Western and Chinese Landscapes

	Western	Chinese
Method:	used models; on site painting; could change	mind's eye, relatively quick, No changes
Virtue:	orginality prized	skill prized
Surface:	entire surface painted	blank spaces
Materials:	oils & canvas	paper/silk & ink
Display:	hang framed paintings picture centered	rolled scrolls 2/3 margin on top = heaven / 1/3 on bottom
Writing:	No writing on paintings	calligraphy on paintings
Perspective:	3-dimensional	2-dimensional
Color:	colors	often just one color
Subject:	only Landscape	landscape + people & water & mountains
Time of day:	~~shawdows~~ shadows	No shadows

71 CHINA SCHOLASTIC PROFESSIONAL BOOKS

ACTIVITY #2
Painting Scroll Landscapes

Overview

The purpose of this activity is to give students an opportunity to see for themselves what was involved in Chinese-style landscape painting. They will better appreciate the skill of the Chinese artist when they have used a brush pen and ink to paint a landscape on paper without having first sketched a picture.

Materials

- Rectangular sheets of off-white drawing paper
- Brush pens, one for each student, and black ink
- Colored construction paper (black, gray, tan for contrast) for mounting
- 2 small paper cups for every 3 to 4 students
- Glue or paste
- Copy book of Chinese art such as *The Mustard Seed Garden of Painting* (Princeton University Press, 1978) or *Chinese Landscape for Beginners* (Sterling, 1993) or examples of Chinese paintings
- Practice paper

Procedure

1. Students should do this activity after working with a brush pen and ink (see Calligraphy Workshop, page 55). However, if a little practice time is allowed, this activity can be done on its own.

2. This lesson should follow a discussion of the principles of Chinese painting, as set forth in the Background Information section. Students should try to conform to Chinese artistic principles. This is a more important goal than the appearance of the final product.

3. Students should use practice paper to experiment with the brush pen and ink, and try drawing compositions of mountains, water, houses, bridges, boats, etc.

4. When a student is ready, provide drawing paper. Students should *not* be permitted to sketch in pencil first, as this is contrary to the Chinese way of painting. They should try to have a mental image of the picture they want to paint before they start. No changes are permitted, so if students make a mistake, they begin again on a new piece of paper.

5. After the students' completed paintings have dried, they should mount them. Apply glue sparingly and evenly to the backs of the paintings. Place them on construction paper so that the space at the top is twice as long as the space at the bottom.

6. Have students write poems about their own paintings. Poems are written in one corner, as part of the painting.

7. Students can sign their paintings with their name chops (see Making a Name Chop, page 58).

8. Display students' work.

Name ____________________

Comparing Western and Chinese Landscapes

	Western	**Chinese**
Nature:		
People:		
Light:		
Materials Used:		
Line & Patterns:		
Writing on Painting:		
Texture:		
Color:		
Story/ Activity:		
Time of day:		

Chapter 6

Family and Culture

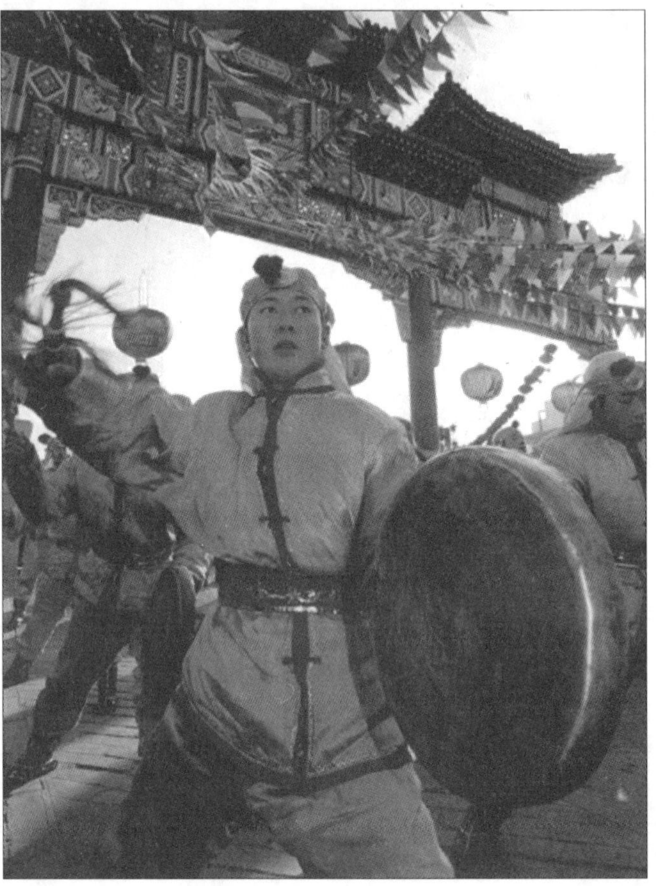

Goals for the Unit

Concepts

1. To understand a society, one must know about its family structure and customs.
2. The family has been the central unit of Chinese society.
3. Confucian philosophy shaped traditional roles within the family. It promoted the group over the individual, age over youth, male over female.
4. Traditional Chinese society was male-centered.
5. Festivals and holidays are often based on religious beliefs and ancient legends.

Skills

1. Analyze how philosophy and religion shape society.
2. Compare different world views.
3. Use artifacts to broaden knowledge of religious beliefs and myths.

Background Information

The Family in China

The family has been the single most important unit in Chinese society since ancient times. The basic ideas of government were derived from analogies to the family. The head of the household was the eldest male. He made all the decisions. Younger members of the household were expected to obey him without question.

Chinese households ideally comprised several generations living together, an extended or "joint" family consisting of grandparents, the eldest son, his wife, and their children. Wealthy families lived together in large compounds that included other sons in the family, their wives and children.

The family consisted of persons with the same surname. When a woman married, she left the family of her birth and took the family name of her husband. Her children, in turn, belonged to the family of her husband. Children, in particular male children, were important because they carried on the family name. Only someone with the family name could make offerings to the spirits of departed ancestors, the spirits who watched over their descendants.

The importance of the family is shown by the fact that the family name comes first. Chinese usually have three-character names. The first is the family name; the next two comprise the personal name. Traditionally, children born in one generation, especially males, were given a "generation name" as part of the personal name. All cousins of a particular generation shared this generation name. Only one character out of the name's three characters differed from person to person. Within the family, people seldom referred to each other by name; rather, they addressed and called each other by relationship, for example, Big Brother, Second Sister, Third Uncle.

Clan was the next level of family. All persons having the same surname are believed to be related. In China there are rather few family names. Despite this and the huge 1.2 billion population, it is still considered improper for people of the same surname to marry.

In China two principles guided family relationships: age over youth and male over female. With age came honor, prestige, and status. One of the most important concepts in traditional society was that of "filial piety"—the greatest loyalty and respect is owed by a child to a parent. If the oldest surviving member of the family was the grandmother, she often exercised great power within the family. However, the oldest adult male could always overrule her. Males were the head of the household, made the decisions, and handled all family business.

Marriage was a family affair, not a matter of love. The bride and bridegroom might never see each other before the marriage. A union advantageous to both households was arranged with the help of a go-between. The purpose of the marriage was to have sons to ensure that the family line continued. If it also resulted in further prosperity for the family, so much the better. Although Chinese parents loved their children and tried to establish matches they felt would be happy ones, this was not their primary concern.

The Role of Women in Traditional China

The most important person in the family was always male, and in particular, the oldest male. Only males could present offerings to the ancestors at the family shrine or temple, and males were responsible for tending the graves of the ancestors. Only men could inherit property.

Chinese society was polygamous: men were free to have more than one wife if they could afford it. The principal wife had certain prerogatives; secondary wives, or concubines, also had rank in the household. The most common reason a man took a concubine was if his first wife did not have a son. In theory, he could divorce his first wife, which would be a great shame for the divorced woman, but it was more common to take a second wife instead.

A new bride moved to her husband's home. If her husband was the eldest son, she was expected to obey her mother-in-law without question. Most mothers-in-law, despite their own identical experiences, treated daughters-in-law as servants. Tyrannical mothers-in-law are a popular subject of Chinese fiction. Having sons was the single most important way a woman could improve her status, but she was still subject to the will of her mother-in-law until the day the older woman died.

If a woman became a widow, she was expected to stay that way. Remarriage was considered dishonorable. Nor could she return to her own family, no matter how young a widow she was. Once married, she belonged to her husband's family, even if she remained childless.

In ancient times, Chinese women seem to have had somewhat more status than in more recent times. You can see tomb figures of court ladies astride horses, playing polo, and upper-class women were at least educated and fairly independent. The practice of foot binding, an indication of women's status as purely decorative, did not begin until the Song Dynasty, a time of increased prosperity when women were not so necessary as members of the workforce. More than 3,000 years of Chinese history had elapsed before the practice started in the upper classes and gradually spread to all social classes. It was outlawed in the 20th century.

Holidays and Festivals

Although Chinese now use the Western solar calendar for everyday activities, traditionally, Chinese marked time by the lunar calendar. Thus, Chinese holidays and festivals occur at different times each year in our Western calendar. Note that many of the dates on the lunar calendar are "double," meaning that the number of the month and day are the same. For example, the Dragon Boat Festival occurs on the fifth day of the fifth month, the Weaver Maid Festival is on the seventh day of the seventh month. Perhaps in ancient times this had some sort of powerful significance. Listed below are the most important holidays and festivals.

The Chinese New Year

As with most agricultural societies, Chinese people celebrated festivals based on the agricultural cycle. The Chinese New Year comes at the beginning of this cycle, around the first part of February (1st day of the 1st month—a new moon). This is the most important holiday of the entire year. Families, even those living far apart, get together for dinner on New Year's Eve. At midnight, people set off fireworks, and continue to do so on New Year's Day. Everyone visits relatives and friends.

Because the holiday marks a new beginning, debts must be paid before it occurs. People buy new clothes and clean their shops and homes in preparation. Decorations are hung in homes, shops, and along the streets. Once the actual new year has arrived, lion and dragon dances and other street celebrations take place, and special foods are eaten.

Although businesses normally close only one to three days, the New Year season actually lasts until the Lantern Festival, held on the 15th day of the lunar new year, when the first full moon of the new year occurs. Colorful lanterns in traditional designs are bought to decorate homes, restaurants, and temples, and children even parade through the streets carrying them.

Qing Ming Festival

Qing Ming Festival, which comes in the spring, honors the dead. Families visit cemeteries to sweep their ancestors' graves. They might also repaint the inscriptions on the headstones.

The Dragon Boat Festival

The Dragon Boat festival usually occurs in June (the fifth day of the fifth month) and combines a traditional celebration with an exciting boat race. Qu Yuan was a poet and official who drowned himself in the 3rd Century B.C. in protest against a corrupt government. According to legend, villagers first tried to rescue him, then, when they realized he had drowned, beat drums to scare fish away and threw rice into the river to keep them from eating Qu Yuan's body. Today festival activities reflect these events. The boats are elaborately decorated with the heads and tails of dragons. Drums, emulating the commotion of the villagers' attempts to rescue Qu Yuan, accompany the boat race. People eat packets of glutinous rice, meat, and other ingredients wrapped in bamboo leaves.

The Weaver Maid Festival

Held in the summer (seventh day of the seventh month) the Weaver Maid festival dates back to Chinese folklore more than 1, 500 years old. According to one legend, a weaving maid once led a lonely life at her loom. Her father, the Heavenly Emperor, feeling sorry for her, allowed her to marry a cowherd from across the Milky Way. But after the wedding, she neglected her weaving duties, so the emperor ordered her to return home. She was allowed to visit her husband only once a year—on the seventh day of the seventh moon. People offer fruit and burn incense in the open air, where they can look at the night skies for the two stars that represent the cowherd and the weaver maid.

The Mid-Autumn, or Moon, Festival

One of the major festivals of the Chinese calendar, the Mid-Autumn, or Moon, festival, takes place in September (the 15th day of the eighth month, which is always a full moon). The festival commemorates the lady of the moon, Zhang O. The story is that around 2,000 B.C., the famous archer and architect Hou Yi performed extraordinary services for the gods. As a reward, he was given a pill of immortality. His wife, Zhang O, who was very curious, found the pill and swallowed it. She immediately soared up to the moon, where she remains to this day. On the night of the Moon Festival, Zhang O is supposed to be at her loveliest.

During the festival, people eat special pastries called moon cakes, round pastries filled with sweets such as lotus, sesame or bean paste, fruits, or preserves. Another Moon Festival story has it that at the end of the despised Mongol Dynasty, a Chinese patriot smuggled messages of rebellion in each moon cake, and thus enabled the Chinese to overthrow their invaders.

On this occasion, parents allow children to stay up late, watch the moon and eat moon cakes. Lovers also arrange trysts and watch the moon together; its roundness symbolizes wholeness.

Confucius's Birthday

Confucius's birthday, also celebrated in September, is an important state celebration in Taiwan, where special ceremonies are held at the Confucian Temple. Recently, the celebration has also been held in Shandong, Confucius's native area.

ACTIVITY #1
New Year's Celebrations

Overview

To develop an appreciation for the way the Chinese celebrate their biggest festival, students will participate in the Chinese New Year in a variety of ways: making model firecrackers, lucky characters, lanterns, paper cuts, pictures of the new year animal, as well as finding their own birth years on the Chinese zodiac.

Red Envelopes

During the New Year celebration, friends and relatives greet each other with the phrase, "Gongxi facai," pronounced, "Goong-shee fah-tsai." It means, "I wish you happiness and prosperity." You might post this sentence and have students practice saying it. A child's playful rejoinder to this greeting is "Hongbao nalai," pronounced, "Hoong-bao nah-lai," which means, "Hand over the red envelope." Small red envelopes containing money are traditionally given to children by married relatives.

We give our students red envelopes with candy inside or something else of real value, like a homework pass!

Firecrackers

Materials: red tissue paper, toilet-tissue spools, gold and silver paint (half-pint cans are more than enough for the entire class), gold paper, cardboard, red construction paper, glue and scissors.

Procedure

Each student can make one of these.

1. Cover toilet-tissue spools with red tissue paper. Glue the seam. Tuck in ends.

2. Decorate with gold or silver paint.

3. Put a loop of red construction paper on one end.

4. Attach each "firecracker" to one link in a red construction paper chain. The construction paper chain can be any length.

5. At the top of the chain, attach either a cardboard circle covered in gold paper and decorated, or a cardboard cutout of a lucky character covered in gold paper or painted gold. Attach a loop at the top for hanging.

6. Hang the strings of firecrackers near the door and from the ceiling.

Lucky Characters

Materials: Lucky characters (at right); red construction paper; gold ink

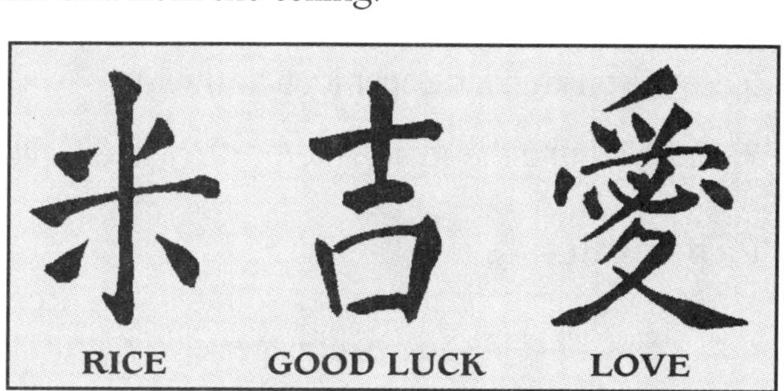

Procedure

1. Write lucky characters on squares of red paper in gold ink.

2. Hang them upside down. The Chinese word "dao" means both "upside down" and "arrived." When you put the word upside down, it means that the good thing wished for will arrive. It's wise to display a note showing that you know the character is hanging upside down with a short explanation.

Spring Couplets

Materials: red paper, gold ink, and pens or gold markers

Procedure

1. Cut paper into rectangles approximately twice as long as they are wide.

2. Encourage children to choose a saying from the list of traditional wishes for good fortune:
   - Wishing you luck and prosperity.
   - Satisfactory marriage with many children.
   - May you enjoy continuous good health.
   - May you continue your advancement in education.
   - May all that your heart desires come to you.

3. Alternatively, children might make up their own wishes.

4. Holding the paper vertically, students should write their sayings in gold in English.

5. Hang these rectangles on the door of your classroom.

Lanterns

Materials: red construction paper; gold and silver paint; glue and scissors; strips of paper shorter than the construction paper

Procedure

1. Fold the construction paper in half, horizontally.

2. Cut parallel slits from the fold, upward and downward to about 2 inches from the edges. Open the paper so that the fold bulges toward you.

3. Decorate with gold and silver paint and/or cut fancy designs into the slats.

4. Connect the right and left sides of the paper to make a cylinder, with the decorated side facing out.

5. Glue two paper strips inside as braces so that the lantern will bulge out. Glue the seam.

6. Put a construction paper loop at the top.

7. Hang around the room, and/or carry in a New Year's parade.

Paper Cuts

Materials: gold or red paper squares, *not* from construction paper (origami paper is best); red, white, or gold squares of paper or construction paper

Procedure

1. Fold thinner paper squares on diagonal to make a triangle.

2. Fold again at right angles to the first fold to make a small triangle four layers thick. Notice where the folded sides are.

3. Sketch a design first or cut freehand. Be sure to cut through all four layers at once. The more intricate the design, the more interesting the paper cut. You may cut along folds or along the outside of the design. If you cut along the folds, be careful to keep the folds connected.

4. Unfold carefully, one fold at a time. If you don't like the design, refold and continue cutting.

5. Press the completed design flat.

6. Mount with glue on red or contrasting paper, or attach to a window without mounting.

The Chinese Zodiac

Materials: Zodiac Spinner Wheels (page 80); brass fasteners

Procedure

Hand out copies of the Zodiac Spinner Wheels to students. Have students cut out each wheel, and cut out the two windows on wheel #1. Fasten the two wheels together with a brass fastener. Invite students to a picture of each animal to the wheel. Students can etiher draw them or cut the pictures out of magazines.

Activity #2
Moon Festival Mystery

Materials

Moon cakes (almond cookies), Message in the Mooncakes story (on next page), index cards.

Procedure

1. Use the story below to create the Moon Festival Mystery. You will need to modify it so that it has the same number of sentences as there are students in your class.

2. On index cards, neatly print one of the sentences from the holiday story in a substitution code: each letter in the encoded sentence is one before the letter it represents in alphabetical order (e.g. cat= bzs). Number the cards so that you can order them easily later.

3. For fun, write one of the following sentences on one side of each red index card: It is the hour to drive the barbarians back to Mongolia! Revolt on the night of the full moon!

4. Hide the cards in your students' coat sleeves, books, and cubbies while they are out of the room. When they return, they will find their cards. Eventually someone will figure out it is a code and how to decode. You can tell them, if they don't figure it out themselves.

5. When all the students have translated their sentences, ask them to read them in order. By that time, everyone will know what the activity is about and why you have given it to them. The reward is moon cakes, cookies, and milk!

6. Encoding all those sentences is a chore so you can laminate the deck of cards and put them away for next time.

MOON FESTIVAL MYSTERY

The Mid-Autumn Festival comes on the 15th day of the eighth lunar month. The Chinese name for the festival is Zhong Qiu Jie. This is a day to worship the moon god. It is also the birthday of T'u-ti Kung, the earth god. This festival celebrates the end of the year's hard farming work. People express their gratitude to the moon, which stands for all of heaven. They are also grateful to earth, symbolized by T'u-ti Kung, for the good fortune of the past year. Round "moon cakes" are eaten. Some are filled with nuts and dried fruits.

As part of the celebration, people gaze at the moon. The Chinese believe in praying to the moon god for protection, family unity, and good luck. Many think the moon is the largest, roundest and brightest of the year on that day. After dark, people like to sit outside sipping jasmine tea, eating, talking ,and moon gazing.

During the 13th century, the Moon Festival had another meaning. Rebels were preparing to overthrow China's Mongol leaders of the Yuan Dynasty. To be successful in a rebellion, the support of the villages was needed. To communicate secretly, the rebels slipped messages about the uprising into the moon cakes. The legend says that these messages contributed to the success of the rebellion.

Chinese Zodiac Spinner Wheel

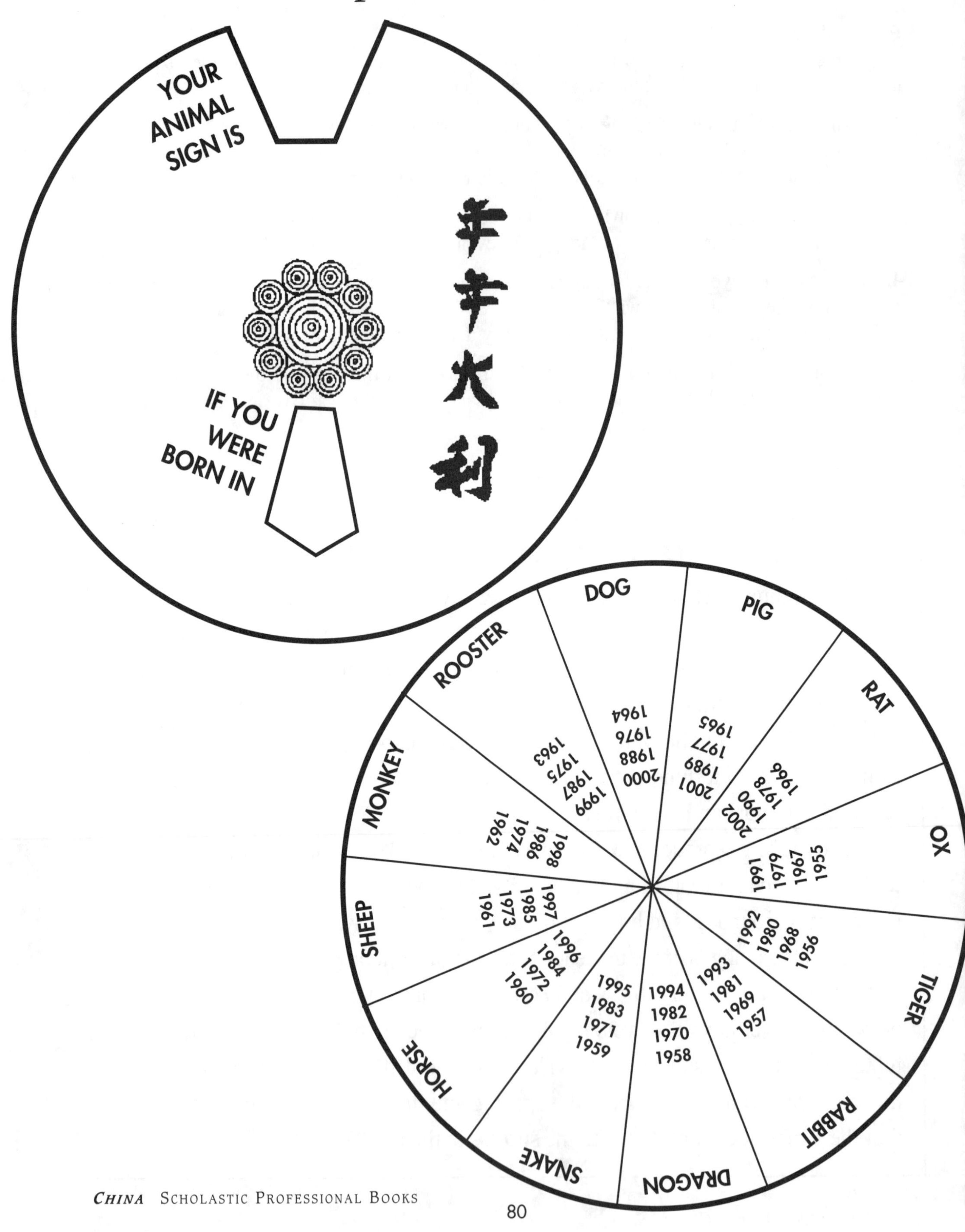

CHAPTER 7

MODERN CHINA

Goals for the Unit

Concepts

1. Governments and laws evolve in response to the needs of people.
2. Governments may act to preserve their own authority.
3. Like personal conflicts, national conflicts are resolved in a variety of ways.
4. Economic systems are ways of organizing the production and distribution of goods and services.
5. The political system of a country may be involved to a greater or lesser extent with the economic system.

Skills

1. Using graphic organizers (charts) to compare ideological systems
2. Using graphs to learn about population growth.
3. Using literature to enhance the study of modern Chinese history.
4. Using dramatization and role-play activities to deepen students' understanding.
5. Using current events to extend students' understanding.

Background Information

An Overview of Modern China

The period known as Modern China has no distinct starting date. We prefer to begin with the Opium War between China and Great Britain in 1840. That event marks the beginning of Western imperialism in China. It also was the first shock to the proud and complacent Chinese under the Qing. Change was inevitable, whether or not people realized it then.

Between the Opium War in 1840 and the return of Hong Kong to China in 1997, the events and leaders, ideologies, and problems of China are extraordinarily complex.

Important Events

China was constantly at war for more than 100 years following the Opium War. These were both civil wars and wars against foreign aggression. The suffering of the people was immense, for war exacerbated the natural disasters of flood, drought, and famine.

The most important events are: the Opium War and imperialism in China by Western powers and Japan (unequal treaties); the 1911 internal revolution led by Sun Yat-sen; the Northern Expedition to reunite China; the struggle between the Nationalists led by Chiang Kai-shek and the Communists led by Mao Zedong (Mao Tse-tung); Japanese aggression in China and World War II; the victory of the Communists in 1949; Land Reform; the Great Leap Forward; the Cultural Revolution; Tiananmen; and the pro-Democracy-Human Rights movement in China today.

The Opium War resulted from Chinese attempts to halt British exports of opium to China. Britain began the trade in order to stem the flood of silver currency from Britain to China. The British bought tea from China, but China under the Qing was not interested in buying from Britain. Opium turned the monetary tide in favor of the British. When Commissioner Lin (Lin Zexu), a hero in modern China, burned the British stockpile of opium, war resulted. The Chinese lost. Unequal treaties, in which Western powers and the Japanese assumed virtual control over areas of Chinese territory and economy, were the norm. The first of these, the Treaty of Nanjing, ceded the island of Hong Kong to the British.

The 1911 revolution led by Sun Yat-sen overthrew the Qing Dynasty and ended the 2,000-year-old imperial system. But it did little else to change the lives of people. If anything, the political uncertainties under regional warlords which erupted following the demise of the empire made people's lives harder. Sun's principles of democracy, nationalism, and livelihood never became reality. Nevertheless, change came gradually to China.

The Northern Expedition of 1926–1928 was a largely successful effort to reunite China. The Nationalists under Chiang Kai-shek and the Communists initially were united in this military campaign that came from the south to Beijing. Many regional warlords were either defeated or convinced to join the forces of the Republic. However, in Shanghai in April 1927, Chiang carried out a secret plan to get rid of the Communists. Thousands of Communists and their supporters were killed and arrested. Those who survived went underground or fled to more remote regions.

What followed was a decades-long struggle between the Nationalists led by Chiang Kai-shek and the Communists led by Mao Zedong. Although Chiang headed the recognized government of China in his capital at Nanjing, the ongoing civil war with the Communists consumed both manpower and energy. One of the most famous events of this period is the 6,000-mile Long March of the Communists as they retreated from Jiangsu in central China to Yanan in the northwest. The 10 percent of the marchers who survived the grueling yearlong trek won a place in legend as well as history.

Japanese aggression in China in the 1930s before the actual beginning of World War II was marked by savagery. Events such as the Rape of Nanjing show the Japanese military in the worst possible light. The Japanese soldiers were indoctrinated with the idea that the Chinese were subhuman, and it was, therefore, acceptable to treat them savagely. Despite fierce Chinese resistance in the coastal cities, Chiang felt he could not defeat the Japanese and that retreat to the interior was his only recourse. In addition, he regarded the Communist threat as greater than the Japanese one. This attitude cost him the support of many Chinese who saw the Communists as more patriotic in the struggle against the Japanese.

After the American victory over Japan in 1945, the civil war in China resumed in earnest. The victory of the Communists in 1949 was at least as much due to the weariness of the Chinese people at the corruption and incompetence of Chiang's government as it was to an embrace of the ideals of Communism.

The Communist Land Reform in the 1950s resulted in the confiscation and redistribution of land to China's peasantry—a move widely popular among that group. The power of the landlord class was destroyed, and Communist-led peasant associations enabled the government to extend its control to the countryside. Redistribution was the prelude to a program of collectivization (collective ownership) of the land.

The Great Leap Forward in the late 1950s was supposed to be an all-out push to bring China's industrial production up to the level of European countries. The money to do this would come from the agricultural sector, newly restructured into communes. The results of this nationwide effort were disastrous: 20 million people died of starvation in the greatest man-made famine in history; the backyard furnaces which were supposed to raise China's steel output produced steel of such poor quality as to be essentially worthless; large areas were deforested to feed these small but inefficient furnaces, which in turn caused soil erosion, flooding, and more famine.

The Cultural Revolution was Mao Zedong's last attempt to arouse the revolutionary fervor of China's youth, and incidentally, to harass members of the Communist party whom Mao wanted to target, namely those who felt expertise was more important than ideology. Mao unleashed forces which quickly got out of hand. The results are still felt in China today. China lost uncounted cultural treasures as anything old or "feudal" was destroyed. A whole generation of skilled people were persecuted, imprisoned, and sometimes killed, or else sent to the countryside to do menial work. Schools were closed, resulting in a generation with little or no formal education. Perhaps the most long-lasting effect was the trauma caused by the violence and disorder. It left a generation of people, including some of China's most prominent subsequent leaders, with a fear of any mass movement.

In June 1989, the Chinese government violently suppressed a group of Chinese students and workers protesting in Tiananmen Square. This event marked the Chinese government in the eyes of the world as a repressive regime and gave impetus to the pro-Democracy-Human Rights movement in China today.

Ideologies

Ideologies that influenced the Chinese were not limited to Marxism. Chinese intellectuals and government officials were attracted to various political and economic systems, including our own.

The most defining ideology of the 20th century was, in fact, nationalism. In contrast to the traditional attitude, that being Chinese was a cultural identity, the modern view was that the nation should be the focus of the loyalty and identity of the people within its boundaries, and its welfare should be of paramount importance. This ideology was the only concept that all the different factions in China agreed upon.

Beyond that, there were a number of competing ideas. Socialism, communism, and its Chinese variation, Maoism, all believed in government ownership of the means of production, including land, and in government control of the distribution of wealth. Mao's contribution was in proposing the peasants as vanguards of the revolution, instead of the proletariat, the urban workers. His idea proved instrumental in the ultimate victory of the Chinese Communists.

In addition to ideologies of the left, there were republicans who espoused representative government headed by a president; parliamentarians who wanted to emulate the British system; fascists who advocated a one-party system of government that also regulated industry and finance; and those who advocated laissez-faire capitalism, an economic system in which factories and businesses are privately owned and operate for profit.

Although the victory of the Chinese Communists in 1949 seemed to decide the issue of ideology, it is perhaps easier today to see influences other than socialism, including those of China's own past, at work in the policies of the present Chinese government.

Problems in China Today

Population control is one of the most serious problems in a country with China's huge population base and geography. Meeting the needs of so many people for food, drinking water, housing, health, education, and jobs is a primary challenge for the Chinese government. Furthermore, urbanization and industrialization are diminishing the already meager acres of farmland. The age-old problem of deforestation continues, despite government efforts to plant trees. As China's population increases and spreads west and south, more forests are cleared for timber, fuel, or agriculture. Such environmental degradation only worsens soil erosion, and the heavy load of silt carried by the Yellow and Yangtze Rivers. This, in turn, adds to the danger of flooding and complicates efforts at water control with dams. Increasing development and industrialization have expanded the demand for electricity and resources. This in turn has led to massive projects such as the Three Gorges Dam on the Yangtze River. Furthermore, pollution from factories and automobiles threatens the health of people and ecosystems. China's economic strength and tradition of hegemony in East Asia have resulted in foreign relations policies emphasizing prestige, and a role for China as a world power.

Talking About:
Dramatizations and Role Plays

Children love to pretend they are other people. In the pre-school and early childhood years, they do it in play. In the upper elementary and high school grades, students still enjoy playing roles, and it serves as a way for them to practice socialization skills. At this point, however, we can introduce more structure into dramatic play and use it to expose learners to social studies content and concepts, to develop sensitivity to different points of view, and to provide opportunities for students to apply new information. Here are a number of ways we've used dramatization and roleplay in our curricula.

Scenes and Plays

When we studied religion in the New England colonies, we read Arthur Miller's *The Crucible* aloud. When we learned about the Declaration of Indpendence, we read scenes from *1776*. At various other times, we've used short plays on historical events we found in magazines such as *Junior Scholastic*. Usually we use a "Reader's Theater" approach: students say their lines with scripts in hand. Students who are otherwise reluctant to participate willingly take part in dramatic readings.

If we can't find scenes to read aloud, we have groups of students write them. We might pose a problem that has to be solved in an original scene, or we'll read half of a short story or tale from the culture we're studying and ask groups to take turns improvising a scene that finishes the story. Also, we ask students to imagine the effects of a historical event on ordinary people, or to write the script of a conversation between historical figures.

Role Plays

We use role play when we want students to stay with a character or a set of characters for a period of weeks or months. Our goal is to help students understand that historical events and geography affect the lives of ordinary people.

In the China study, we would first select a time period. In a project about the imperial period, students might first choose between scholar-gentry or common people. Then within the class of common people, students might choose to be merchants, peasants or craftsmen. We would provide a list of family and given names from which they would choose, and maps so they would know where their characters lived. With this information, they could start to make connections between the geography and lifestyle of their characters. Then we ask students to make visual representations of their characters. Students have done this in a variety of ways: they themselves have become their characters; they've also made dolls, portraits, and collages.

After the class has spent more time studying the subject, we fashion another menu of projects related to the characters and the topics we have covered. If we were studying geography, for example, we'd have the students make maps of where their families lived, draw pictures, or make models of their homes or towns. Then we would go on to learn about some other aspect of imperial China, like family roles or philosophy, and then we'd present several ways students might write or create something that would express the relationship between their characters and that information.

Activity #1
Discussion Questions on Modern China

Overview

The following are discussion questions for events mentioned in the Background Reading. You can use these questions at the end of your unit on Modern China to review and wrap up your unit. You can also use them as writing and research prompts for students. Have groups of students or individuals research and answer any of the following questions.

Discussion Questions

1. What were the reasons for the deterioration of the Qing dynasty? What did the Qing do to try to stop the decline? Why did these efforts fail?
2. What was the 1911 revolution? What were the results of the 1911 revolution? Who was Sun Yat-sen and why is he honored in China?
3. What was the Northern Expedition? What happened in 1927 in Shanghai?
4. In what ways did the Nanjing government fail?
5. What was different about Mao's view of revolution in China?
6. Why did the Communists emerge victorious in the civil war?
7. What is "land reform" and why did the Chinese do it?
8. Why was the Great Leap Forward a failure?
9. What was the Cultural Revolution? What effect did it have on China?
10. What happened in Tiananmen Square in 1989? What were the results?
11. Why does the Chinese government suppress dissent in China today?
12. What is the reason for China's one-child policy?
13. What are the biggest problems facing China today?
14. Do you think China today is different from its traditional past? Explain your answer.

Activity #2
Comparing and Contrasting Ideologies

Overview

Students use graphic organizers to compare and contrast ideologies.

Goals

1. Students gain understanding of the advantages and disadvantages of Confucianism as China entered the modern world.

2. Students see how Communism fit with previous ideologies of China: Confucianism and Legalism.

Materials

Advantages and Disadvantages of Confucianism graphic organizer (page 92); Running a Country: Confucianism, Communism and Legalism graphic organizer (page 93)

Procedure

1. Give students time to read over the two charts.

2. Ask for several students to explain what the charts are about.

3. Ask students how organizing information on charts like these is different from looking at it in paragraphs in a book. What can you understand more clearly when you organize information this way? In what ways is a book better?

4. Ask other questions that use the information for the chart directly, so that students develop some facility with locating information. Example: If a government is based on Confucian principles, who will the leaders be? (educated scholars who pass a test)

5. Use the first chart, Advantages and Disadvantages of Confucianism when discussing the initial period of contact with the West. Ask students: Who benefited most from Confucianism? Who benefited least? Divide the class into groups representing different groups in Chinese society (scholars, laborers, peasants, soldiers, women). Have students in each group decide whether there were more advantages or disadvantages for their group. What would they like to see change? What should stay the same? Have each group share their ideas with other groups to see where points of agreement and conflict arise.

6. Discuss how Communist ideology fits into the Chinese tradition. What points are similar in Communism and Confucianism? What points are similar in Communism and Legalism? If you were a Communist cadre, how would you use this information to implement these programs?

7. Discuss each event using the two charts as a touchstone. Example: Why do you think Mao's Great Leap Forward, in which land was turned over to peasants and farmed collectivelly was a failure? (This attempt at mass collectivization of the farms conflicted with Confucian values: Ancestral land became parts of large collectives. People had to travel miles from their villages to go to work. Family members were separated.)

Follow-up Activities

Researching Key Events in Modern China: Either as individuals or in groups, have students research the following events in modern Chinese history: land reform; Great Leap Forward; Let One Hundred Flowers Bloom; the Cultural Revolution; the Pro-Democracy Demonstration in Tiananmen Square; economic reform. Each group should try to answer basic questions about the events: What was it? When did it take place? What was its effect on the Chinese people?

Teaching Strategy

Working with Grids: If your students are able to work comfortably with grids, try assigning an activity where they have to read a passage and take notes by constructing their own grids. This is a good way to introduce the notion of how nonfiction text is organized. Students might pay attention to section headings, topic sentences, and subordinate details. They might be asked to determine how most of the paragraphs in the reading are organized. What is the reading about? What will you compare and contrast? What aspects of all of them may be compared?

ACTIVITY #3
Land Reform

Overview

The goal of this activity is to allow students to experience personally the inequities of the landholding system in China. In order to do this, use students' work spaces to represent landholdings.

Before You Begin

Have students read accounts from 2 sources *The Dragon's Village* by Chen Yuan-tsung (Penguin Books, 1980) and *Growing Up in China, 1930-1949* by Katherine Wei and Terry Quinn (Holt, Rinehart and Winston, 1984), pages 70–73. The first describes the grinding poverty of a typical Chinese village, while the second describes the wealth and feudal power of the landowning gentry.

Procedure

1. If you have tables, divide them into two areas. One area should be a prime location. At the tables in that area, seat only two or three students per table. Seat all the other students at the tables in the second area. Give them a school task, one that requires writing, like answering questions from a book, so that the crowded students are uncomfortable. Do not allow them to move to the roomier tables.

2. After at least 15 minutes, discuss with the students how they feel. First address their physical discomfort or comfort, then the justice of the arrangement. Get students to articulate their feelings of anger or resentment.

3. Ask students to talk among themselves to find peaceful ways to change the situation. For each possible solution, have the "privileged" students decide whether they will accept it. If none are accepted, ask the crowded students to decide (but not act out) what they will do next. Permit the "privileged" students to respond.

4. At this point, have students take their normal seats. Draw the correlation between what they just experienced and land reform in China. On the basis of their readings and the experience they have just had, compare and contrast wealth and poverty in China.

Teaching Strategies

1. Tips for Successful Role Playing Activities: Which students do you choose to be the "priviledged landlords"? Generally, avoid the very popular or unpopular students because the outcome is too much affected by how the other students feel about them. Find kids who don't arouse strong responses, and who don't have traits that might make them targets.

2. Helping Students React and Respond: Students tend to get pretty emotionally involved in this activity. How forthright should you allow students to get when criticizing the "landlords"? Students need to remember they are playing a role, and should stick to the part they are playing, whether landlord or peasant. This keeps the dialogue from getting personal.

Follow-up Activities

Point-of View Story: Have students write historical fiction from the point of view of a Chinese involved in land reform. You may assign them the character they represent (either landlord or peasant), or allow them to choose. Students should include both the historical events as well as their emotional response to them.

ACTIVITY #4
The Population Problem

Overview

China has the largest population in the world: 1,218,800,000 according to United Nations figures for 1995. Despite the decline in the birthrate to 1.1 percent, China's population is still growing rapidly because of its large base. China's policies on population control have been widely publicized in this country and have been the subject of much criticism. The graphs and questions provided in this activity are meant to help students understand the issue.

Goals

1. Gain understanding of the issues relating to population.
2. Use graphs to get information.

Materials

China's Population at a Glance (page 94); China's Birth and Death Rates; Population Density; How China's Population Has Grown; China's Population Growth Since 1950

Procedure

1. Have students examine the four graphs. Ask them to write down on notebook paper the titles of each; next to the title, have them record the years covered by the graph.

2. Use math to calculate the population increase each year, then each day. First, divide the difference between successive bars by the time elapsed (example: 1.21 billion minus 1.18 billion equals about 20 million). To get the yearly rate, divide by 5 (20 million divided by 5 equals 4 million). To get the daily rate, divide the yearly rate by 365 (4,000,000 divided by 365 equals 10,958 people per day, between 1990 and 1995).

3. Have students look at the bar graph How China's Population Has Grown to determine population increases for each interval, and compare the number of years it took for that increase to occur.

4. Next, have students look at the bar graph of China's population growth since 1950. Again, ask them to ascertain population growth and patterns of growth.

5. By examining the graph of birth and death rates, students can try to correlate them with political events. Ask them to look at what has happened to the birth rate since 1984, when the one-child policy went into effect. See if they can account for the rise.

6. Students can use the population density graph to project what the density will be by the year 2000.

7. Using the information above, plus readings found in the Resources, discuss the following questions:

- What effect would rapid population growth have on the people of China?
- Do you think China has solved its population problem? Explain your answer.
- How would you propose to deal with the problem of China's increasing population?

ACTIVITY #5

Mao Zedong and Martin Luther King, Jr.: Two Ways to Change Society

Overview

In the 1949 Revolution, Mao Zedong defeated Chiang Kai-shek's Nationalist forces and drove them off the mainland. But feudalism did not disappear overnight: the gentry still owned the land and peasants remained under their yoke until, one by one, rural villages were "turned over" by peasant associations. In the first reading, Mao clearly endorses the violent overthrow of the landlord class as a necessary aspect of revolution. In the second, Martin Luther King, Jr., explains his rationale for using nonviolent resistance to change society. Both selections can be particularly powerful reading for young adolescents who may themselves face the choice of whether to deal with conflict violently or nonviolently.

Goals

1. Read and understand primary source materials
2. Identify the two ways of resolving conflict
3. Apply each way to other historical (or current) situations

Materials

Reading, "The Necessity of Violence," from *Selected Works of Mao Tse-tung, Volume 1* (Foreign Language Press, 1965) also available online at www.blythe.org/mlm/main-page.html.; Reading, "Martin Luther King Explains Nonviolent Resistance," from *The Martin Luther King Companion* (St. Martins, 1993)

Procedure

1. Using the techniques that are appropriate for your group, read the two articles.

2. Discuss the readings. Focus the first part of the discussion on understanding the main points of each. Try to have students explain difficult concepts such as King's statement, "To the degree that I harm my brother...to that extent I am harming myself."

3. Choose a historical conflict you have already studied (e.g. the start of the Civil War, the Montgomery bus boycott). Briefly review the facts of the event.

4. Challenge the students to think about what might have happened if the groups involved in the conflict had used the opposite strategy (e.g., the South had nonviolently protested

Lincoln's election, or the black people of Montgomery responded violently to the arrest of Rosa Parks). Discuss. If students are too vague about historical conflict, use a local conflict, or make one up involving willing class members.

Follow-up Activities

Journal Writing Prompt: Assign a journal entry in which students write down their thinking about how change should occur in society. Should nonviolence always be used? Should violence? What are the advantages and disadvantages of each? Allow time for the journal entries to be shared. If learning to write essays is a goal for the year, perhaps the journal entry could serve as the brainstorming stage for an essay. By the time students need to organize their thoughts about the topic, they have already read, discussed, and interpreted their two sources. Students might also be assigned to write short summaries of the two. These could be used in their opening essay paragraphs.

Extension Activities

***The Last Emperor*:** This 1987 Bernardo Bertolucci film does a terrific job of reviewing the events of 20th-century China. We like our students to be familiar with the history first so they can enjoy the pleasure of recognition when they see a graphic representation of what they have learned in another mode. If the students know a little bit about each of the following, they will enjoy the film more: the Manchu Dynasty; the Empress Dowager Tzu Hsi; the Emperor Pu Yi; the Kuomintang; the Sino-Japanese War; and the Cultural Revolution.

Vocabulary Bingo: During our study of the 20th century in China, we found there were many events and terms we wanted our students to know a little bit about. These eventually found their way onto flash cards and became the vocabulary for the unit. To check the students' mastery of these, we played Vocabulary Bingo: Rule or fold a sheet of paper into a 5-by-5 inch grid. Have students randomly write one term in each box, so that each student has a different sheet. You should have a complete set of cards at the front of the room. Put your set in a plastic bag. When you choose a card, call out the definition rather than the term. Make markers out of bits of paper, or instruct students to put an *X* in every box that's called. (In the next game, they can put another letter in the box to mark it.)

Current Events: Begin a clipping file of articles relating to China. These days most deal with economic or human rights issues. Encourage students to make use of what they already know as a context for understanding the articles. Make time for students to lead their own discussions about some articles. We rotate leadership, and have two discussions on two articles in a class period. Students read an article before class and write down questions they have about its meaning and issues they'd like to discuss. We sit away from the class and monitor how well the leader chairs the meeting. We look at elements such as how the leader used his voice, how responsive he was to the comments of the other students, how well he encouraged all the students to participate. We intervene only when necessary. Sometimes, we jot down interesting responses students have, and post them on construction paper with the articles, crediting the speakers.

Name ______________________________

Advantages and Disadvantages of Confucianism

Advantages	Disadvantages
It provides stability and predictability; everyone's roles are well-defined.	There is no incentive for any kind of change and innovation.
It emphasizes family values.	There is not a lot of freedom for individuals.
Government officials have to pass exams; they are educated.	Not everyone has access to an education.
It emphasizes personal integrity and responsibility.	There are few protections from abuses. Courts are supposed to be fair, but they may be arbitrary.
There were early technological advances.	There is stagnation in technological advances.
There is respect for elders (filial piety) and ancestor worship.	These rules restrict and devalue young people and women, who are oppressed. Practices such as foot binding and arranged marriages are the rule.

Name ____________________

Running a Country: Confucianism, Legalism, and Communism

Confucianism	Legalism	Communism
The government exists to rule for the benefit of the Chinese people; the emperor models correct behavior for all to imitate.	The government exists to maintain or expand the borders of the state.	The goverment is to serve as an overseer, to provide the benefits of shared efforts to all; it is to manage the economy for everyone.
There is no representation of the population.	There is no representation of the population.	The government is supposed to be made up of ordinary people, but it is not.
Inequalities between people, classes and genders are accepted as they are defined; Those in power act justly.	Power rests with the government	People are supposed to be equal
Educated scholars who passed literary exams are supposed to lead.	Leaders rule according to strict application of the laws.	CCP cadre and party members are supposed to lead.
It emphasizes stability.	It emphasizes stability.	It emphasizes change.
Ideology is most important.	Practicality is most important.	Ideology is most important.
People should be enlightened through education.	People should be controlled with rewards and punishments	People should be indoctrinated through education.
It emphasizes the welfare of the group over individuals.	It emphasizes the welfare of the state over individuals.	It emphasizes the welfare of the group over individuals.

China's Population at a Glance

Name ____________________

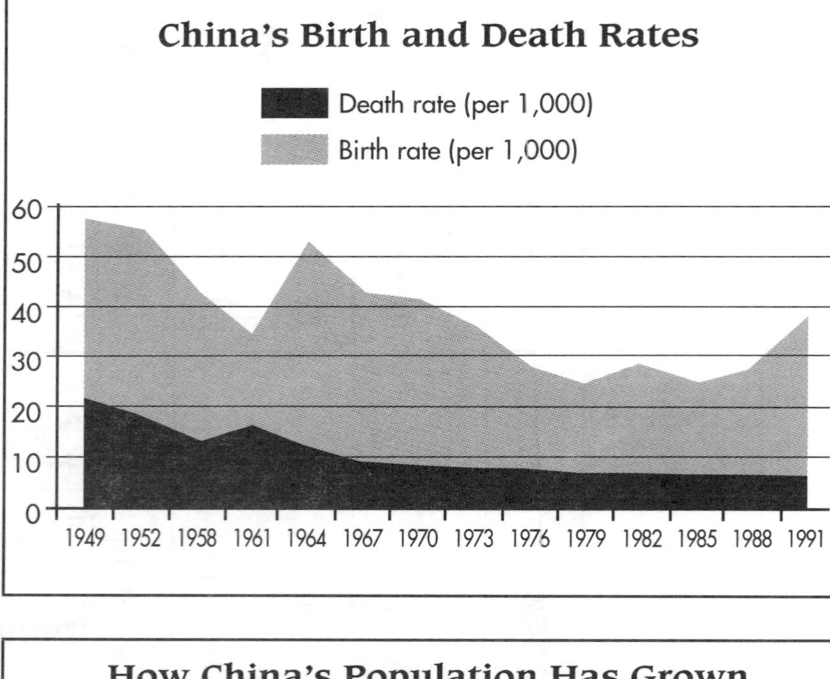

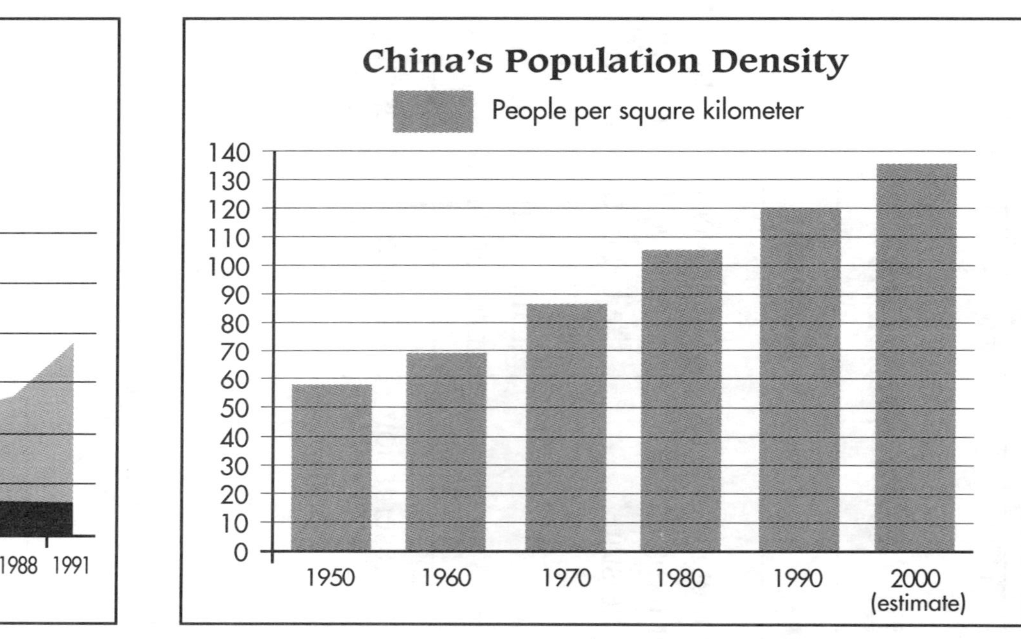

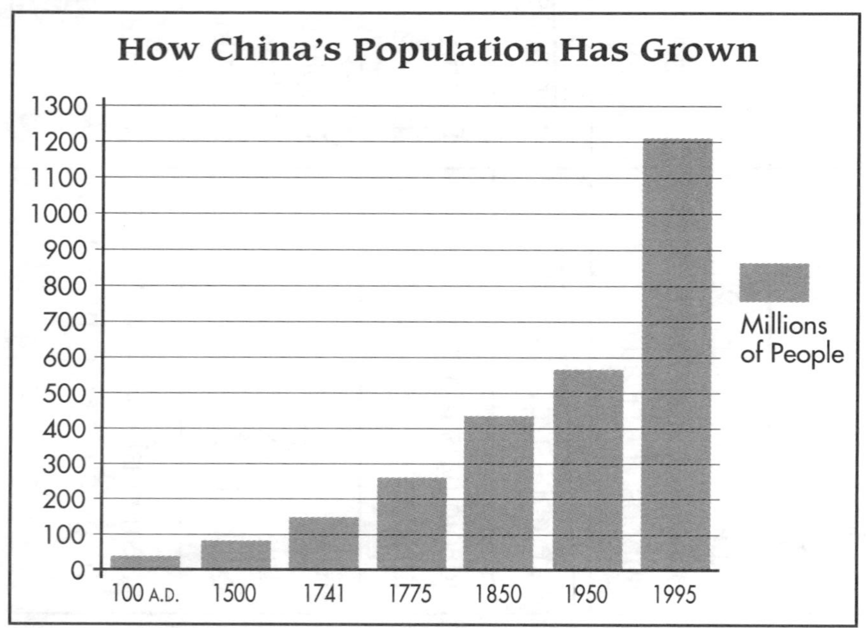

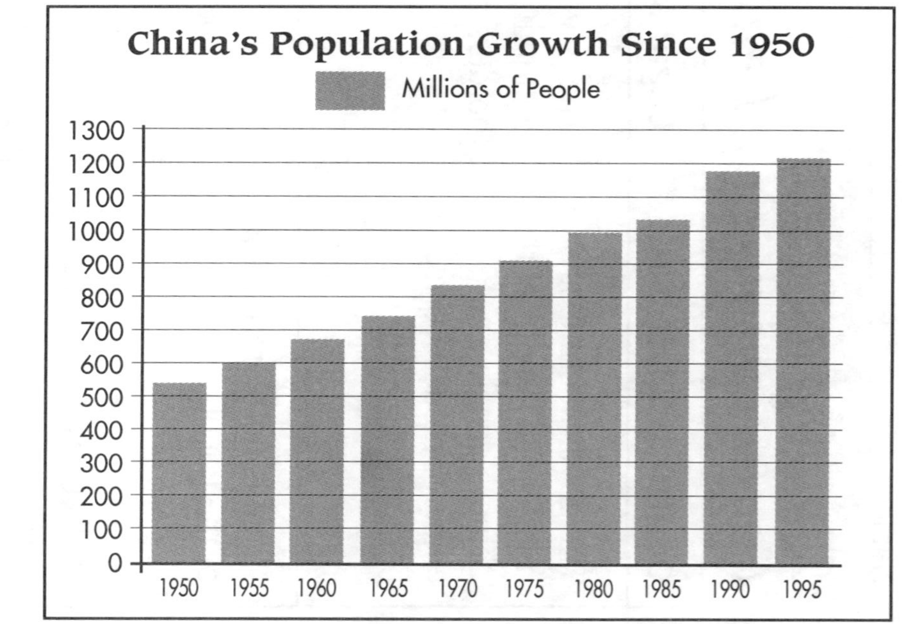

RESOURCES

Books, Videos, and Websites

General Reference & Atlases

The Cambridge Encyclopedia of China edited by Brian Hook (Cambridge University Press, 1991)

China by Catherine Charley (Raintree/Steck-Vaughn, 1995)

China by Colin Cheong, edited by Elizabeth Berg (Gareth Stevens, 1997)

China by Kim Dramer (Children's Press, 1997) *Games People Play Series*

China by Philip Steele (Crestwood House, 1994) *Discovering Series*

China by Julia Waterlow (Raintree/Steck Vaughn, 1997) *Country Insights Series*

China by John S Major (Harper Collins, 1989)

China A History in Art by Bradley Smith and Wan-go Weng (Harper and Row, 1972)

Chinese:16 Cultural Activities For K-6 Children by Marlene Bird, & Barbara Schubert (Reflections and Images, 1976)

Chinese Village Cookbook by Rhoda Yee (Yerba Buena Press,1975)

Chinese Cooking: An Illustrated Guide by Ayako Namba and Grace Z. Chu (Barrons, 1981)

Fun With Chinese Festivals by Tan Huoy Peng and L. Chuen (Heian International, Inc., 1991)

The Genius of China: 3,000 Years of Science, Discovery, and Invention by Robert Temple (Simon and Schuster, 1986).

Hands On: China by Margaret Elmer & Charlotte Beall (The Children's Museum, 1991)

Mooncakes And Hungry Ghosts: Festivals Of China Carol Skepanchuk and C. Wong (China Books & Periodicals, 1991)

An Outline of Chinese Geography by Chi Chung (Foreign Languages Press, 1978)

Scholastic World Cultures: China by Daniel Chu (Scholastic, 1986)

Nystrom Desk Atlas (1997 ed.) Rand McNally Classroom Atlas, (1997 ed.)

Rand McNally Quick Reference World Atlas (1997 ed.)

The Contemporary Atlas of China (Houghton Mifflin, 1988)

Note: Many atlases do not feature a map of China, or place it in such as way that the entire middle section is unusable. The most detailed and usable map is in the Quick Reference World Atlas

General Nonfiction and Biography

The Great Wall of China by Leonard Everett Fisher (Macmillan, 1986)

Chingis Khan by Demi (Holt, 1991)

The Little Lama of Tibet by Lois Raimondo (Scholastic, 1994)

A Young Painter: The Life and Paintings of Wang Yani by Zheng Zhensun and Alice Low (Scholastic, 1991)

Novels, Folktales, and Poetry

Cat and Rat: The Legend of the Chinese Zodiac by Ed Young (Henry Holt, 1995)

The Empty Pot by Demi (Holt, 1990)

The Good Earth by Pearl S Buck Enriched Classic Series (Washington Square Press, 1973)

Gung Hay Fat Choy by June Behrens (Children's Press, 1982)

Journey of Meng: A Chinese Legend by Doreen Rappaport, & Ming-yi Yang (Dial Books for Young Readers, 1991)

Lon Po Po: A Red-Riding Hood Story from China by Ed Young (Harpers, 1989)

The Magic Tapestry by Demi (Holt, 1994)

Maples in the Mist: Children's Poems from the Tang Dynasty Translated by Minfong Ho., Illus. by Jean and Mou-sien Tseng. (William Morrow & Co., 1995)

Films and Videos

PBS series on China: "China in Revolution," "China Under Mao," "Born Under the Red Flag" Also "Heart of the Dragon"

To Live by director Zhang Yimou

The Last Emperor, dir. Bernardo Bertolucci, 1987, Columbia Pictures Corporation, 160 min., PG-13

WEB SITES

General Web Sites

www.aweto.com/china
Dozens of links about history, government, geography, sports and entertainment, languages and festivals, and more. Also, hundreds of links to other China sites.

www.execpc.com/~dboals/chin-ja.html#CHINA/JAPAN
Eighty-five China links about every aspect of Chinese history and culture.

www.socialstudies.com80/china.html
The Social Studies School Service's online resource list; some virtual tours and some good democracy movement resources.

www.askasia.com
The Asia Society's site includes material for teachers and students, as well as a wide range of information and resources.

History and Geography

www. members.aol.com/Donnclass/Chinalife.html
A breezy, brief, but very accessible overview of daily life and beliefs of the ancient Chinese.

asterius.com/china/
Includes information about all the dynasties.

www.-chaos.umd/history/welcome.html
A detailed chronology and history of China, nicely indexed.

www.darkwing.uoregon.edu/~felsing/cstuff/history.html
In addition to the usual historical information, lists links to articles on the history of science, women, more.

sun.ihep.ac.cn/tour/china_tour.html
An index to several dozen articles, each on a particular province in China; and excellent resource for a geography reseach project.

Chinese Culture and Literature

www.ChinaPage.com/eng1.html
A great collection of classical poetry, including the famous poets of the T'ang.

www.geocities.com/RainForest/3458/Cph.html
Links to sites about Chinese philosophy including Confucius, I Ching, Lao Tsu, Chuang Tzu, and Mencius; also, literature, calligraphy, and literature.

www.chinapage.org/china.html
A virtual museum and concert hall including poetry, painting, calligraphy, language, literature, and more.

www.houstoncul.org/culdir
Several dozen e-pamphlets, well-written and illustrated with photographs about topics from archery to chopsticks, opera to pottery; a great resource for research projects.

falcon.jmu.edu/~ramseyil/mulchinese.htm
A list of juvenile books about China and Tibet.

Other

www.kn.pacbell.com/wired/China/index.html
Six increasingly challenging web activities for students (and teachers), which enable users to learn about China and to link to other useful sites about it.